For Brian

On the occasion of
your Honorary Doctorate
from U.A.E, or even
U.E.A.!
With love from
Brenda and John

The Story of Holy Island

Kate Tristram studied history at the universities of Oxford and Edinburgh, and is a Canon of Newcastle Cathedral.

She was formerly warden of Marygate House, an ecumenical retreat house on Holy Island, and is an island resident.

The Story of Holy Island

An illustrated history

Kate Tristram

CANTERBURY
PRESS
Norwich

© Kate Tristram 2009

First published in 2009 by the Canterbury Press Norwich
Editorial office
13–17 Long Lane,
London, EC1A 9PN, UK

Canterbury Press is an imprint of Hymns Ancient and Mod-
ern Ltd (a registered charity)
St Mary's Works, St Mary's Plain,
Norwich, NR3 3BH, UK

www.scm-canterburypress.co.uk

British Library Cataloguing in Publication data

A catalogue record for this book is available
from the British Library

978–1–85311–945–3

Typeset by Regent Typesetting, London
Printed and bound in Great Britain by
CPI William Clowes Beccles NR34 7TL

To the people of Holy Island

ontents

Acknowledgements

Very many thanks to all the friends who supported this piece of writing, and especially to Brother Damian SSF, Vicar of the Island, who gave the initial impetus; to Tony and Caroline Glenton and to Geoff Porter for invaluable moral and practical support; to Lilian Groves who read the whole book in typescript; to Barry Hutchinson, Tony Owens, Ian Mills and Ray Simpson for their contributions to Chapter 12; to the many who offered pictures and stories, especially to Elfreda Elford for her unfailing wealth of stories; to all those on the Island and elsewhere who, when they heard I was writing a book, were kind enough to say, 'I'm looking forward to it!'

Abbreviations

Where Bede is used as a source his *Ecclesiastical History* is referred to as EH, and his *Life of Cuthbert* as VP.
The anonymous *Life of Cuthbert* is abbreviated as VA.

Illustrations

Illustrations at the front of the book and on chapter opening pages are drawn from the Lindisfarne Gospels. They include a panel from the St Mark 'carpet-page' (page iii), portraits of the four evangelists, each of which appeared at the beginning of their gospel (pages ix, xi, xvi and 163), and many intricate designs based on birds and dogs.

From the Book of Durrow, which is believed to have been written on Holy Island 20 years before the Lindisfarne Gospels, are drawn symbols that were used to represent the evangelists (pages i, v, 95 and 141).

Photo sections

1   View from the Island to the mainland with the snow-capped Cheviot Hills in the distance. Mesolithic people would have seen this as a flat plain.
    Photo: Rachel Crick

2   The statue of St Aidan in St Mary's churchyard on the Island. The sculpture is by Kathleen Parbury, 1958.
    Photo: Lilian Groves

3   An impression of a youthful St Cuthbert from a window in St Mary's church, Holy Island. Designed by Leonard Evetts.
    Photo: Lilian Groves

4   A bronze cast of a wooden sculpture of St Cuthbert by Fenwick Lawson, now standing in Lindisfarne Priory.
    Photo: Rachel Crick

5   St Cuthbert's Island, where he was first a hermit, seen from Holy Island at high tide.
    Photo: Rachel Crick

6   The Wheel Cross by Fenwick Lawson, showing the face of St Cuthbert. Now in the Gospels Garden on Holy Island.
    Photo: Lilian Groves

7   The sculpture by Fenwick Lawson called The Journey, depicting the monks carrying the body of St Cuthbert away from the Island. Now in St Mary's church, Holy Island.
    Photo: Lilian Groves

8   A view of St Mary's church in relation to the ruined Benedictine priory.
    Photo: Rachel Crick

9   The Rainbow Arch: the most striking feature of the ruined Benedictine monastic church.
    Photo: Lilian Groves

10 In the foreground the embankment on which the wagonway brought limestone to the kiln.
    Photo: Enid Riley

11 The later set of lime kilns, near the Castle.
    Photo: Lilian Groves

12 All that now remains of the jetty from which ships took the powdered lime.
    Photo: Lilian Groves

Map of Holy Island

with places mentioned in the text

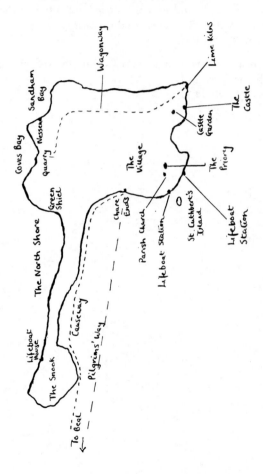

Introduction

In a local bookshop I once came across a paperback which promised to tell me about the ghosts of Northumberland. I read the first chapter and learned that the ghost of St Cuthbert is *often* seen in the ruins of Lindisfarne Priory. Puzzled, I looked at the second chapter, which told me that the ghosts of the Lindisfarne monks are *often* seen fleeing across the sands from the Vikings. I closed the book. I have lived on the Island now for 30 years; I have wandered around it and crossed the causeway at all hours of the day and night; I have never seen them. I have known most of the people who have lived on the Island during these 30 years and I have never met anyone who has had these experiences. Later I opened a reputable magazine which had an article on Holy Island. It told me that a thousand eider ducks nest on the Holy Island of Lindisfarne. In fact not a single eider duck nests here for they are far too sensible: they are ground nesting birds and we have foxes. They all nest on a real island a few miles across the sea.

Why do people write and read this kind of thing? Among our hordes of visitors we sometimes meet those who believe it. To them Holy Island is not a real solid place of real people; it lives in a kind of fairy-tale. We have known those who have said it would be great fun to live in a little wooden hut on Holy Island in the winter, like the saints, so peaceful. The only answer to that can be: try it!

So this book about the Island's story aims to stick to reality, as far as our sources can reveal it to us. At all ages the people of the Island (including our saints) are real people, owning property or other possessions, concerned about the success of their work, keeping on their feet in hard and slippery times, maintaining loyalty and good relationships as best they could. I write as one who is privileged to live here among them, and I have used the words 'here', 'our' and 'ours' quite freely.

The first ten chapters of the book attempt to tell the story from the beginning up to the closure of the second monastery at the Reformation. The last two chapters bring it up to the present day, but in them I have had to be very selective and deal mainly with what has been new during the years being described. I have neither the knowledge nor the space to give a complete history of the social and economic factors affecting the Island people during that time. That would require another book, and a different author.

So I offer this book to the Island and its people, with my love.

I

Misty Beginnings

In 8000 bc Holy Island was not yet an island, but just part of
a flat coastal plain. We can picture a group of men near what
is now the Island quarry working at shaping their stone tools.
These Middle Stone Age people were the first humans who trod
the soil of the future Holy Island. We know about them through
investigations in the 1980s by the archaeology department of the
University of Leicester, which at the time worked on the Island
for a few weeks every year. Archaeologists Deirdre O'Sullivan
and Robert Young describe an initial find of a scatter of flints
and worked stones left behind when the stone tools were made.
Some 381 pieces were found, and so a detailed investigation was
undertaken in 1983 and 1984, which discovered no fewer than
2,500 pieces from the Middle Stone Age (8000–4000 BC), the
New Stone Age (4000–2000 BC) and the Bronze Age (2000–
1000 BC) approximately. This has now become known as the
'Nessend find'. But among these pieces of stone there were very
few finished tools. So this, we conclude, for several thousand
years was the site of a tool workshop; the finished tools were
taken away to be used elsewhere.

Our archaeologists commented that prehistoric man was skilful and discriminating in his choice of materials. If the stone-
worker found a 'good' piece of stone he could remove several
'flakes' which could then be shaped for various purposes. But

the archaeologists found several pebbles which had had only one flake removed and then were discarded. This suggests that the craftsmen found them not up to standard.

Mesolithic (Middle Stone Age) men were hunters, fishermen, food gatherers, so they needed knives, arrows and spearheads. When the prey was caught they needed to prepare their catch for use. Some bevelled pebbles, which earlier were thought to be for scooping limpets off rocks (the limpets for bait rather than for human consumption), are now thought to have been for scraping the inside of sealskins, where a sharper tool would damage the soft skin. Later, in the New Stone Age, when people cleared the forests and began to farm, axeheads were needed and also more sophisticated arrows and spearheads.

If Mesolithic people had looked around, what would they have seen? To the west their vision was bounded by the Cheviots, the oldest rock in the area, formed by volcanic activity some 400 million years ago. To the east they might just have been able to see the edge of the sea, which was a few miles further out than it is now. Around them stretched the coastal plain, flat except where it was broken by humps, such as the Heugh along the south side of the present Island, Beblowe Hill where Lindisfarne Castle now stands, the rock at Bamburgh where Bamburgh Castle now stands, the headland where the ruin of Dunstanburgh Castle now stands and the Farne Islands. All these are the easternmost parts of the Whin Sill, a rocky outcrop running across much of the north of England, which is a mere 300 million years old. The North Sea at this time had no outlet to the south: roughly from the modern city of Nottingham southwards it would then have been possible to walk across to the continent. Mesolithic people did not cultivate the soil: they had no need to, since nature provided abundantly. They could hunt animals ranging from the majestic red deer to smaller mammals such as hares; the sea and the rivers provided seals, waterfowl and a great variety of fish. Berries, nuts and several kinds of edible plants added to the diet. Very few remains of dwellings have been found, but one Mesolithic hut excavated near Alnwick showed a building of timber and grass which could have held a family group of six to eight people. Some remains of less substantial buildings have led to the conjecture that the men of the family might have gone on longer hunting expeditions and 'camped out'. It is also conjectured that a number of families would have joined together for bigger social and cultic occasions.

Described like this it can sound like a comfortable existence! But the sea-level was beginning to rise . . .

The rise of the sea was very slow. Some 18,000 years ago the whole region was still under the last of the Ice Ages. The hills were ice-capped and much of the lowlands was covered with sheets of ice. The reason why Palaeolithic (Old Stone Age) people have not been mentioned is that it is extremely unlikely that they were able to live in Northumberland, so they remained in the warmer regions further south. By about 13000 BC Northumberland was largely ice-free. About the year 10000 BC it is thought that sea-levels were about 30 metres below the present level. Gradually the low-lying coastal plain was drowned. By about 6500 BC Britain as a whole had lost its land-link with the continent and was an island. By about 4000 BC the coast of Northumberland was established more or less as it is, so by that time Holy Island had become an island. Since then the coast has been subject to local changes here and there, as it still is in places, including Holy Island, where the sea is longing to cut us into two and down to size.

4000 BC is the beginning of the Neolithic or New Stone Age, so it is likely that these were the first people to live on the Island as an island. Unfortunately we have, so far, very little evidence of Neolithic people here although, because archaeology is so exciting and unpredictable, that could change at any moment. We have just enough to know that they did live here: a small amount of material from the Nessend find, a single microlith from near the Castle, a fragment of a Neolithic axehead in the village. Recently archaeologists had to examine part of the main street of the modern village in preparation for building new houses there. They found postholes which by radio-carbon dating were from 3685–3365 BC. This is the best evidence so far for Neolithic activity actually on the coast. Fortunately inland it is a very different picture. From the near mainland there have been substantial discoveries, which will at least suggest to us some details about the life of our Neolithic forebears. These discoveries have been made in the Milfield plain which, as the crow flies, was not too far from the Island for such seasoned walkers as we imagine our ancestors to have been.

In general in the Neolithic period the big changes were the introduction of arable farming and the domestication of animals. Of course these changes happened gradually, with hunting/gathering still continuing alongside. But it is speculated that these new activities brought with them a major change in human thinking because they involved, for the first time, actual ownership of land and animals. Before this, in the Mesolithic Age, people may have seen themselves as simply one mobile and food-seeking species among others. The new methods of farming brought with them competition for resources, hostility through competition, the emergence of wealth for some, the formation of an elite and ruling class. The first permanent graves were constructed: does that signify human control of landscape? New technologies meant not simply larger populations but also the emergence of new crafts: the first pottery was made, tools changed their shape and use, the cultivation of cereals led to grinding flour and making bread.

These are the practicalities of life. Humans have also enquiring minds and spiritual hopes. The Milfield plain, which was originally a glacial lake, filled with sand, gravel and clay brought by water and ice-sheets, has the largest concentration in Britain of 'henges'. A henge is simply a circular monument, no longer existing above ground but identifiable from the air by marks in the soil. The circle consists of a mound with a ditch on the *inside*: this detail shows that the henges were not for defence. Occasionally individual graves are found in the vicinity, but henges are not cemeteries. It is usually thought that they were for ceremonial purposes. The Milfield North Henge has an inner circle of posts; other henges have no obvious internal features. The archaeologist Clive Waddington has suggested that the eight henges of the Milfield area formed a processional route: each of the henges has two entrances opposite each other, indicating that people could walk through; he believes that the route began at Milfield North Henge and wound its way to finish at Yeavering Henge. Of course we do not know what thoughts and activities happened on the way. But this may have been a cultic act involving a lot of people, and perhaps the Neolithic Holy Islanders joined in.

Nothing yet has been discovered on the Island belonging to the Bronze Age (except a few stones in the Nessend find) or to the Iron Age (1000 BC onwards). During the Roman period (c. 50–410 AD) again there are no discoveries. It may well have been that there was a fishing village here of local people, Britons of the tribe called Votadini. But so far there is no evidence. So the story of the Island moves on to the post-Roman period.

In the early 400s the Britons, appalled and feeling unprotected, saw the Roman legions depart. From Rome's point of view this was necessary to protect Rome itself and the Mediterranean heartlands of the Empire, now threatened by the 'barbarians', that is, Germanic tribes from northern Europe. But although the Britons had not welcomed the Romans when they first invaded they had got used over the centuries to being 'Roman' themselves. They asked for the legions back, and were told 'See to your own defences'. The traditional enemies, the Irish ('Scots') and the Picts, continued to raid, but the greatest change was caused by the coming of a new enemy, the Anglo-Saxons, Germanic peoples from north Germany and south Scandinavia. According to one story these early English were actually invited in by the Britons to help against the raiders. But then they turned against their hosts and settled, first in the south and then moving northwards, gradually turning what had been lowland Britain into the country eventually known as 'England'. Many of the Anglo-Saxons who came are thought to have been simply farmers looking for good land and prepared to settle among the local Britons. But Germanic society was 'heroic' in the sense that its leaders were a military aristocracy headed by a king; their aristocrats cared only for fighting and extending their conquests.

Here in the north-east, during the still misty sixth century, two kingdoms emerged: Bernicia (roughly modern Northumberland and County Durham) and Deira (roughly modern Yorkshire). These two kingdoms, together with other conquered lands, form Northumbria. Its story is dominated by these kingdoms coming together under one ruler and then falling apart again. Bernicia, in the seventh century, was the senior partner.

But one episode at the end of the sixth century should be mentioned because our island features in it. It must be emphasized that very great doubt has been felt by many historians about the historical value of the source of this story, which is a collection of earlier material compiled by 'Nennius'. He first gives genealogies of the kings of Bernicia and Deira, beginning with the god Woden, the essential ancestor of most Anglo-Saxon royal houses and gradually moving to names that can be recognized as historical. For the royal house of Bernicia the human ancestor was Ida, and among his sons was Aethelric who, according to Nennius, was besieged with others on the island of Medcaut. Medcaut is none other than our Holy Island under its British name, of which the meaning is unknown. The Anglo-Saxon leaders were trapped there, says Nennius, by four British kings, of whom the leader was Urien, King of Rheged (Carlisle). The Anglo-Saxons fought vigorously but seem to have been saved by the assassination of Urien by his own side: he is said to have aroused the jealousy of the other Britons. This Urien is a major figure in some early heroic poetry, so if there is a historical basis for this story it suggests that the Anglo-Saxons in this area first established themselves along the coast, where an effort by the British to dislodge them failed.

One of the Anglo-Saxon leaders mentioned here is Aethelric, said to be the father of Aethelfrith, who was certainly a historical figure, with whom we are on firmer ground. He flourished from the 590s until 616, when he was killed in battle. An extremely competent war leader, he drove the Britons back in all directions, united the two kingdoms of Bernicia and Deira by forcing the Deira claimant, Edwin, into exile, and so became the 'architect' of the Kingdom of Northumbria. When Aethelfrith was finally killed in battle by Raedwald, King of the East Angles, who supported Edwin, Aethelfrith's children fled into exile. The eldest son, Eanfrith, is said to have gone into Pictland and married there. The second son, Oswald, aged 12, and his little brother Oswiu, aged four, went into exile on the western coast of Scotland. Both of these will be important in the story of Holy Island.

But back in Northumbria, in all the years that Oswald and Oswiu were growing up and living among the Irish in western Scotland, King Edwin was ruling over both Northumbrian kingdoms. Although he was a cousin of Aethelfrith they had been mortal enemies. In earlier days Edwin had had to find refuge where he could; his last bolthole had been the court of East Anglia under King Raedwald. Aethelfrith tried, first by bribes and then by threats, to get Raedwald to kill Edwin. He nearly succeeded, but Raedwald happened to tell his queen about the whole matter and she persuaded him that it would be a very dishonourable thing to kill a guest. At that Raedwald, taking Edwin with him, led an army against Aethelfrith and surprised him as he was returning from a battle against the Britons of North Wales. Aethelfrith was killed and Raedwald established Edwin on the throne of Northumbria.

Edwin ruled for 16 years, 616–32. He proved to be a good, strong king. His reign does not directly affect the Island in any way that we know, though he came near to it when he stayed at his royal settlement at Yeavering. But the fact that he became the first Christian king of the north, and the nature of the missionary effort in his reign, most probably affected the way St Aidan did his missionary work a few years later.

Edwin became Christian as a result of his marriage to the Christian Kentish princess Aethelburh. (Bede's *Ecclesiastical*

History now becomes our main source. See EH Book ii Ch. 9.)
She brought with her a chaplain, Paulinus, one of the Canterbury monks of St Augustine's foundation. Edwin had agreed
that he would be allowed to preach the gospel freely. Paulinus
travelled often with the royal party and preached to the crowds
who came together at the King's various centres. When they
were at Yeavering, at the foot of the Cheviots, Paulinus is said to
have baptized several hundred people in the River Glen there.

Edwin took longer to consider the Christian faith for himself.
But on the day that his first baby, a daughter, was born he also
escaped a murderous attack on his own life. An assassin came
with a poisoned dagger but a faithful thegn, Lilla, thrust his
own body between that of the king and the assassin's knife and
died. In thankfulness for these two events Edwin allowed his
newborn child to be baptized. Her name was Eanflaed and she
was 'the first of the Northumbria race to be baptized'. We shall
meet her again a little later in the story.

Meanwhile the king could not proceed to a matter as serious
as a change of religion without consulting his nobles. What happened when he called this conference is one of Bede's best-known
stories (EH ii 13). Paulinus was invited to speak and two others
in particular swayed the meeting. One was an unnamed noble
who compared this life with the king's hall in winter, warm and
light. In flies a sparrow out of the darkness through one door
and then, after a brief time in the light, out again through the
other door into the dark. If, said the noble, this new religion can
tell us more about the time before or after this life let us accept
it. The other main influence was, astonishingly, Coifi the pagan
high priest, who declared the old religion had done him no good
and proceeded to desecrate his own sanctuary by riding up to
it on a stallion carrying a spear (both actions were against the
pagan rules) and ordering the sanctuary's destruction.

So, on Easter Day 627 King Edwin was baptized at York by
Paulinus, along with many of his people. Among those baptized
with him was one we suppose no one noticed, his 13–year-old
great niece. We shall meet her again. Her name was Hild.

But all warrior kings lived on the edge of disaster and this came to Edwin in the form of an alliance against him of Penda, King of Mercia, and Cadwallon, one of the kings of the Britons. Edwin was killed. Paulinus decided that his duty was to accompany the widowed queen and her young family back to Kent, where he stayed. His deacon James remained in the York area to try to support the Christian mission as well as he could. But it seems that there was a wholesale rejection of the Christian faith among the people. To many of them the fact that Edwin was killed would have suggested that the pagan gods of Penda were stronger. They clearly had not taken on board the idea that the Christian God does not guarantee worldly success.

Perhaps then the mass instruction and mass baptisms were not the best way to evangelize. We don't know what Aidan knew of Paulinus but he certainly chose a quite different method.

The death of Edwin was the signal for the return from exile of Eanfrith, Aethelfrith's eldest son. He too was killed. The scene was set for Oswald to re-enter the story.

But first we must go back to Oswald's childhood and youth in exile, and especially to the place that had most influenced him: the island of Iona.

2

Iona, Mother of Lindisfarne

The Irish background

Ireland was never part of the Roman Empire: the Empire's west-wards expansion stopped at the western coast of Britain. This important fact had many consequences. Irish society had never been shaped by Roman culture in any of its forms; never had heard the tramp of the legions, never watched with astonishment the building of Roman towns or Roman roads to connect them, never heard Latin spoken as the native language of the conqueror. Alone among the western Celts the Irish had no inferiority complex towards things Roman, unlike the British, for example, for whom *Romanitas* became a sign of the upper classes and only the peasants continued to speak just Brythonic. The Gauls, another Celtic people, had been so thoroughly Romanized that their native language, Gaulic, died out completely. But the Irish were proud of their freedom from Rome. The earliest Irish Christian writer whose works have survived, a monk named Columbanus, in writing to the Pope explained that he would love to come to Rome to visit the Pope and the tombs of St Peter and St Paul, but that classical Rome meant nothing to him. Nonetheless the Irish were quite well informed about the western parts of the Empire since they both raided and traded across the sea.

So when Christianity came to Ireland it did not come on the heels of a conquering army. How did it come? The writer who said it 'tiptoed in' was largely right. Much of it came from friendly neighbours, principally Britain. The great missionary St Patrick was of course a Briton and there may have been more; it is probable also, since Ireland had relations with both Gaul and Spain, that early Christian influences came from those countries. But we know of one mysterious group of Christians in the south-east of Ireland, Leinster, who asked the Pope directly for a bishop, and Palladius was sent in answer to this request in 431. Were these Christians converted from neighbouring Britain, or were they even Britons who had emigrated (as many Irish were gradually establishing themselves in Wales)? We can't know, but it seems that they had no connection with Patrick and his work up in the north of Ireland.

Fortunately for our understanding of St Patrick two of his own writings have survived, which show us a missionary wrestling with his job. It is clear that he hoped to establish the Church as he knew it, with bishops, priests and deacons, using the Latin language and fully part of the universal western Church. But his writing also shows how he had to struggle with the expectations of a non-Romanized, pre-Christian society where, to give one small example, gift-giving was part of the structure of relationships. Patrick wished neither to give gifts nor to receive them, but to some degree he had to conform. He wished to introduce the idea of consecrated virginity; he had some success among the women, who then found themselves in great difficulties with their own families. He lived in constant expectation of martyrdom. The Christian faith had no easy conquest.

But very soon after Christianity itself arrived in Ireland it was followed by the monastic movement. This had originated in the eastern Mediterranean, in the deserts of Egypt and Syria, among the early monks we call 'the Desert Fathers'. Then a wave of enthusiasm for the ascetic life swept westwards, to Gaul, to Britain, to Ireland. It probably appealed to something in the Irish temperament, but it also fitted well into their social organization. Ireland at the time was a collection of small kingdoms; within each kingdom society was divided into social classes, with kings and aristocrats leading in everything. The most important fact for any individual was his position within the clan, which would fix for him his way of life, his duties and responsibilities. The whole of Ireland lived by farming, mainly cattle farming, though aristocrats did not do any physical work themselves. Unlike Romanized countries Ireland had no towns to form the centre of bishops' dioceses, so the monasteries themselves became the Christian centres. Once the upper classes had been converted to the Christian faith it would have been comparatively easy to turn one or two of the clan's farms into monasteries, with a group of celibate monks in the centre, led by an abbot who was probably a prominent clan member, and still allowing the peasants who worked that land to continue to do so, not requiring them to become monks. Irish monasteries could not be enclosed and apart. Those powerful ascetics who at first sought to live apart usually soon found themselves surrounded by disciples and a large community established in the place of their solitude!

Nuns play a small part in early Irish monasticism. The most famous name is St Brigid, but her story has been so mixed up with earlier legends about a goddess Brig, and further complicated by a wealth of improbable stories about her as a human saint that historians have great difficulty in discerning the outlines of a real woman in the middle of it all. In fact the social system did not make it easy for women to be nuns. They were honoured members of the clan, but the clan was always represented by its principal men. The clan could set apart land, if it wished, for one of its women to found a nunnery, but the land continued to belong to the clan and reverted to it on the death of the mother-foundress. We hear of one or two names of nuns a little later, but there is no tradition to compare with that of the monks.

Of course not all Irish Christian leaders were monks. There were 'secular' (that is, non-monastic) bishops and priests. Current research is uncovering some of their centres by the study of place-names that indicate the existence of a church but not a monastery. However, in the story of early Christian Ireland, post-Patrick, the important leaders and founders, the ones whose names have come down to us, were monks.

Columba of Iona

One of these was the founder of Iona, St Columba, also called Columcille (dove of the Church). We know of him mainly through a beautiful *Life of Columba* written by Adomnan, the ninth Abbot of Iona, writing about 100 years after Columba's death in 597. This book is not what we would call a biography. The author was in a good position to have genuine recollections of Columba, for he was writing within a community of unbroken tradition, living in the same place and cherishing memories of its remarkable founder. He also had access to an earlier piece of writing about the saint, which has not survived. But he was writing *hagiography*, not biography. Because his wrote about a saint his purpose was to show God working in and through his human agent, not to give an orderly and consecutive account of the development of a man. So Adomnan did not assemble his material in chronological order, like a modern biographer; instead he grouped it under three main headings: prophecies, miracles, appearances of angels. It is not possible to know now in which order these occurred. He did indeed begin with a little information about Columba's family and early days, and he closed his account with a moving description of the saint's last days and death. But Columba's years at Iona are not described in sequence.

A further problem in reading this account lies in some of the details of the monastic life. Was Adomnan really able to describe the monastery as it had been a hundred years earlier, or has something contemporary with his own lifetime crept in? It is a relevant question for historians as some of the most valuable sections of such a book are those which contain incidental details of the monastery and its life.

What we may learn of Columba's life is as follows. His father was called Fedelmith and his mother Ethne. He was born, between 519 and 522, into the most powerful section of the most powerful clan in northern and central Ireland, the Ui Neill (sons of Niall), who derived their descent from an ancestor with the remarkable name of Niall of the Nine Hostages. Columba could hardly have been better born. Given also his considerable personal gifts and talents he would without doubt have become clan leader if he had not been destined for the priesthood. This seems to have been a decision of his parents, who sent him in boyhood to be the pupil of a priest called Cruithnechan, then with another called Gemman, and finally as a young man with a famous bishop, Finian, possibly the founder of the early monastery at Moville, or that at Clonard, or both. We are then not sure of what happened for several years. He is said to have been the founder of the monastery at Derry, but possibly this was later in his life, as were some of his other monastic foundations.

In his early forties he left Ireland, travelled north, and eventually founded Iona. His reason for leaving has been the subject of some speculation. Adomnan says he left 'wishing to be a pilgrim for Christ'. The Latin word for pilgrim, *peregrinus*, came to have a particular meaning for the Irish: it was used for a monk who, after a number of years of normal ascetic life in a monastery, wished to make a still further sacrifice for God and to take a further step in asceticism by leaving his own country, his own kin and all his security and going out to the place and work that God would choose and indicate to him. *Peregrinatio* would become a major reason for monks leaving Ireland over the next few centuries, and this could well have been Columba's purpose. But he did not choose the most extreme form of *peregrinatio* in which the monk went right away from his own people and vowed never to return. Columba did return to Ireland a number of times, to visit his monasteries there or to influence a political decision; and when he chose the west coast of Scotland as the site of his monastery he was among friends, for the Irish were busily colonizing that region.

Later, romantic stories were invented about his decision to go. A popular one is that he quarrelled with another abbot over a version of the Gospels belonging to that abbot, which Columba had copied without permission. He refused to give up his own copy. The case was taken to the king, who judged against Columba, who provoked a battle against that king. There are two elements in this legend which have some historical relevance. One is the undoubted fact that Irish monks were very keen on Bible studies, and the right text was important. The other is the remarkable fact that Columba never became a bishop, together with the report that at one time he was excommunicated by a synod, though not for long. It could be that in some way he provoked a lingering suspicion.

Similarly there are legends about his choice of Iona, such as that it was the first place he came to that was out of sight of Ireland, that may not have much historical base.

Under Columba and his successors Iona grew, flourished and founded several other monasteries. Some of these were back in mainland Ireland and included Durrow and Kells; some were on neighbouring islands, though not all sites have been identified. Columba appointed the abbots of his foundations himself and visited them. It is also part of the tradition about him that he did missionary work among the Picts, and some of the most graphic stories, such as his encounter with the Loch Ness monster, occur in Pictland. At a later point Columban monasteries were established among the Picts.

On Iona itself, following the usual Irish practice, the monastery was built in wood. It does not appear that there was a lay village on the island at this time. Lay people certainly could visit as guests for short periods or as seekers for spiritual guidance, but the monks did their own farming and achieved self-sufficiency. The complete lack of lay residents on the island is indicated by the story that, when Columba's death approached, one of his monks commented on the large numbers who would come for his funeral, but Columba said that a fierce storm would arise so that only his community would bury him: no others would be able to be present. There is nothing to suggest a school on Iona or the presence of children, but intellectual activity, especially the copying of manuscripts, is mentioned quite often, and Columba himself is said to have been occupied in copying even on the day of his death. There is no extant Rule of Iona going back to Columba's day. Perhaps he did not write one; in this early and experimental period of monasticism many abbots preferred to be the Rule themselves and deal with situations as they arose. So there are no details of the daily timetable of the monastery, though we may assume that the monks met several times a day to recite psalms, or else recited them as they went about their work, since this is a common feature of monastic life.

Iona and Lindisfarne

After the death of Columba members of his family continued to rule Iona as abbots: in fact, of the first nine abbots, all but one were blood relatives of the founder. Holy Island is particularly grateful to the fifth Abbot, Segene, who ruled 623–52 and sent the first two bishops of the Northumbrians, Aidan and Finan. The connection between Iona and Lindisfarne followed from the death of Aethelfrith (see Chapter 1) and the exile of two of his children, Oswald and Oswiu, in western Scotland. There, in some way, they met the monks of Iona and were taught the Christian faith, converted and baptized. It is not known whether they ever went to Iona but if so, as suggested above, it was not for long periods. There is no likelihood that Oswald and Oswiu received a monastic education (that is, reading, writing and Latin). This would probably have been considered quite unfitting for boys of royal class, who should be educated to bear arms and lead in battle.

So Oswald and Oswiu, to the best of our knowledge, lived among the Irish, learned the Irish language and way of fighting and fought alongside them. But in all probability Oswald always intended when possible to regain the throne of Northumbria and the death of Edwin gave him his chance. With a small army Oswald confronted a larger force at Heavenfield, near the present town of Hexham, and against all the odds he won the day. The story was told afterwards (and if true it must have come from Oswald himself) that before the battle he had a vision of the great Columba (who had been dead for about 35 years), who promised him heavenly assistance in spite of his small army. It is also said that Oswald put a cross up on the battlefield to show that he fought as a Christian. After he won this decisive battle he decided that, like his father before him, he would make Bamburgh his main centre. Then, when he was established as king, he sent a message to Iona requesting a mission to offer the Christian faith to the pagan Anglo-Saxons.

We must suppose that Iona was delighted. Yet, for some reason a mistake was made there in selecting the leader of this new mission. No doubt he was a senior and well-respected monk in his own community. A later tradition names him as Corman, but Bede just calls him 'austerior', a harsher man. Quite what went wrong for Austerior we do not know: somehow he alienated the people; perhaps he was inclined to shout at them. He went back to Iona and declared the mission impossible, blaming the stupidity of the Northumbrians. The community held a meeting at which one monk spoke up. 'Brother, don't you think you went too quickly? If you had been more patient and content to go slowly might you not have got further?' It was virtually an offer to try again, and the speaker was Aidan. The Irish considered that the right size for a mission was a leader and 12 followers. So Aidan was consecrated as a bishop, given his set of 12 monks and sent off to try his own recipe on the Northumbrians.

Aidan arrived at King Oswald's court at Bamburgh in 635 AD. Oswald, who no doubt was delighted to see him, offered him choice of anywhere in the Kingdom for the site of his monastery. After looking round Aidan chose the island the Anglo-Saxons called Lindisfarne, and time would show what an excellent choice that was.

3

Aidan

If anyone wrote a *Life of Aidan* it has not survived. In the anonymous *Life of St Cuthbert*, written by a monk on Holy Island just after the year 700 AD, there is one mention of 'our holy Bishop Aidan'; otherwise the only source is a precious dozen pages in Bede's Ecclesiastical History.

A note about Bede

Bede must be used with care and with some understanding of his purpose and his limitations. He was a lifelong member, from the age of seven, of the split-site monastery of Wearmouth-Jarrow. Of brilliant academic ability, he made full use of the library which the early abbots of that house had built up. His main interest was in spreading knowledge of the Word of God in Scripture, so to him his Biblical commentaries were his most important writings. But his last major work, finished four years before his death in 735, was *The Ecclesiastical History of the English Nation*, designed to show how the gospel was presented and received by the Anglo-Saxons. This work is now his best-known and has led people to think of him principally as a historian. (Bede would have been surprised!) Bede certainly had the instincts of a historian. He collected sources, both in writing from various monasteries and orally from anyone who would tell him a story. He weighed up these stories and often indicated either that he accepted their witness ('so-and-so, an honourable man, told me') or he reserved his judgment ('so they say!').

But Bede would have thought it pointless to seek simply to describe what happened. He was a servant of Christian truth: he wanted to show that Christian faith and life lead to happiness and rejection of these leads to misery. Of course he had access to only limited knowledge. He very rarely left his monastery and could know comparatively little of the lives of the peasants. His interests were in kings, bishops, abbots, queens, abbesses . . . for, after all, these were the people who had most freedom and opportunity to influence others. Bede was familiar with the type of writing now called *hagiography*, the writing of saints' lives, and the conventions of this writing. He knew that the hagiographer was mainly interested in the action of God through the saint, not in the saint's human growth and achievements. So without deception the hagiographer could use his material selectively, since it was not his purpose to give a whole and balanced picture of a person.

Bede wrote within the conventions of his time. All the same, his knowledge of his own time and place, Northumbria in the seventh and early eighth centuries, was unrivalled. Approached critically his work has been the starting-point for all later historians. He admired the Irish monks, especially Aidan; the only thing wrong with them was the way they calculated the date of Easter (see Chapter 7). He admired their total self-giving and dedication to the job and he was grateful for the charity which had spurred them to leave their own country and come to give the gospel to the Anglo-Saxons. One of the loveliest passages in his book is his tribute to the Irish monks when they left Lindisfarne (EH iii 26).

The choosing of Lindisfarne

So Aidan, when Corman (Austerior) had returned from Northumbria and reported failure, volunteered to have a second attempt at converting the unconvertible. Perhaps, for all we know, Aidan had earlier felt a missionary urge. Perhaps, when the Northumbrian mission had first been mooted at Iona, he had

secretly wished to be chosen as leader. Perhaps also he was moved
by the idea of being a peregrinus like Columba (see Chapter 2).
He seems to have had definite ideas about missionary method,
that is, the gentle and patient approach. He remained true to
these ideas in practice.

So he presented himself and his 12 monks to King Oswald,
presumably at Bamburgh, some time in the year 635. We do not
know what route he took to get there. A possible route would
have been by sea to the Firth of Clyde, across land to the Firth
of Forth, then down the coast to Bamburgh. Another possibility
would have been by sea to Carlisle, then across land following the line of the Roman Wall, then northwards by sea. There
are other possible routes. No doubt the king was pleased at his
arrival. They might even have known each other already. We
do not know Aidan's date of birth, or when he joined the Iona
monastery, so he could have been there when Oswald was in the
area in younger days. Oswald invited Aidan to choose a site for
his monastery and he chose the semi-island of Lindisfarne.

No doubt, to monks used to Iona, the thought of living on an
island was attractive, but the choice was sensible, not romantic. Lindisfarne was near the main royal castle of Bamburgh; in
those days the monks could even have walked at low tide across
the sands from one to the other. (This is not possible now as the
pattern of the sand, including patches of soft sand, quicksands
and guts of water, has changed since Aidan's day.) The nearness
of the king's castle was essential, for the friendship and support
of the king was vital to the success of the mission. In the whole
story of the conversion of Anglo-Saxon England no missionary
is known to have succeeded against the wishes of a ruling king.
A king had to be at least neutral, but Aidan was lucky in that
Oswald was positively supportive. Further, since Northumbria
at its greatest extent stretched from the Humber to the Firth of
Forth, Lindisfarne was not on the edge: it was central to Bernicia
and not remote from Deira. It was open and accessible either by
land or by sea: by land at low tide by walking or riding across
the hard ridge of sand connecting it to the mainland, the site of

the modern causeway, and accessible at high tide by boating into the harbour, which was much bigger then than it is now. Most people chose to travel by sea if they could as the sea was safer than the forested mainland, which in those days still sheltered dangerous wild animals, such as wolves and boars, and even dangerous wild people! Aidan, in choosing Lindisfarne, was not looking for a life of remote peace and leisure. As an active missionary he wished to meet as many people as possible. As a mission centre Lindisfarne was better than the mother house of Iona, since access to it was dependent on the tides but not on the violence of the sea. So the monks could be easily reached by visitors and they could easily reach the mainland. The Bishop could visit the king, and the king could and did visit the monastery. In every way Lindisfarne was an excellent choice.

It seems at the time to have been without inhabitants. If the story of the siege of Medcaut (see Chapter 1) is correct the ordinary people may well have fled from the Island and the warring coastland at that time. There is no hint of a lay village alongside Aidan's monastery until the early ninth century: the remains of a farm belonging to that period at Green Shiel near the sand dunes have been uncovered by archaeologists (see Chapter 9). There certainly was a village of laypeople alongside the second, Benedictine, monastery. But the tradition of Iona seems to have been not to have lay people living on that Island, though welcome to visit if they had need. We know that Lindisfarne occasionally welcomed sick people into residence, though normally even these became monks; but no trace has been found of a village.

On first arrival on the Island Aidan and his monks probably began with a 40-day 'Lent' of prayer and fasting, camping out on the site. Our evidence for this is from the story of St Cedd, who had been a boy in the school here. When he founded his monastery at Lastingham we are told that he prayed and fasted on the site, taking only a little food – an egg, a piece of bread, some milk and water – in the evening. Bede explains that he had learned this from those who taught him the faith (that is, Aidan & Co) and that its purpose was to cleanse the site of any evil or

spiritual nastiness. So presumably they did the same at Lindisfarne, aware as they were of the hidden power of the forces of
spiritual evil.

Then they could begin to build. The Irish always built in wood
if they could get it, and no doubt the king's retainers brought
timber over to them from the forested mainland. Probably the
site of their first little wooden church was underneath the eastern part of the nave of our present parish church, and their small
wooden dwellings were grouped in what is now our graveyard.
When the Irish monks left the Island some 29 years later, Bede
comments how few buildings they had: only those necessary
for their community life. They would have had cattle, and the
monks themselves expected to do the work of the farm.

There is no surviving written Rule of Iona or Lindisfarne. It
seems sensible to suppose that at Lindisfarne the monks continued the pattern of the day which they had followed at Iona: a
regular life of prayer in the chapel with recitation of the psalms
at the centre of all services except the Mass, which had its own
shape (and was probably not celebrated every day). In one respect, though, Lindisfarne could not be a copy of Iona: it was the
only Irish monastery we know of to be founded specifically for
mission. Aidan as bishop would head the mission. He appointed
another monk to be abbot of the monastery and look after it,
since he expected to be absent a good deal. Among the Irish it
was not unusual for a bishop to reside in a monastery in which
another monk was abbot. To continental Christians this would
have seemed strange, since to them a bishop was indubitably in
charge of everything in his diocese and could not be under any
other authority. Bede finds it strange and picks it out for comment. But to the Irish, with their lack of Roman background, the
whole situation was different. Aidan probably did not consider
himself to be bishop of a 'diocese', that is, a territorial area. He
was bishop of the Northumbrian people and could travel freely
among them. It seems that the strategy in his head as he pon-
dered the mission to his huge area was to found monasteries,
dotting them from place to place so that, in the absence of any

parish structure, they would serve as Christian centres. He did found other monasteries, daughter houses to Lindisfarne, but the sites of most of these are unknown.

The school

It was probably in the very early days of the settlement at Lindisfarne that Aidan founded a school with 12 English boys. They were to be trained up as monks, priests, missionaries, even bishops. The fact that they were English suggests that from the beginning Aidan intended an eventual transfer to local leadership: English leaders for an English church. Iona had indeed sent a further group of Irish monks when it became clear that Aidan's monastery was established and that he was not going to return like Corman. But Iona could not do this forever. We think that the school Aidan founded was the first school ever in Northumbria. The boys had to undergo a culture change, possibly even a culture shock. The Anglo-Saxon people, as 'barbarians', were non-literate before they became Christian, whereas Christianity was a literate religion from the very beginning. (Barbarians must not be thought of as 'savages'; they had a considerable culture of their own, including an inscriptive form of writing known as runes. But a book culture was entirely new to them.) So the boys in school, in learning to read and write, had at the same time to master a foreign language, Latin, the language of every book they could obtain. Even the Bible was available to them only in Latin translations. But books were both expensive and heavy, since the only material was parchment, made from skins of sheep, goats or, preferably, calves. It followed that a great deal had to be learned by heart.

The first task in the school, the syllabus for the Reception Class, would be to learn by heart the whole Book of Psalms, of course in Latin. This was the foundation of Christian education. The Irish monks, like all monks, had a special love for the Psalms. There could be no better prayer book since God had given it in the Bible. It contained inexhaustible material for meditation and all human needs found appropriate expression somewhere in the Psalms. The monastic services consisted largely of the recitation of Psalms and, once learned, they were carried in the head for the rest of a monk's life. Some monks indeed were so fond of the Psalms that they attempted to say the whole Psalter each day privately as they went about their work, in addition to the Psalms they recited in the chapel.

Of course, when the boys began to learn the Psalms they would not yet know any Latin, but to master Latin as a language was essential, for the goal of Christian literacy was to read and understand the Scriptures. For potential missionaries more learning by heart was desirable: the Gospels, so that all the traditions about Jesus were readily available as they talked with the pagans; the moral laws of the Old Testament that they thought still applicable to Christians; then as much of the rest as they could manage. Some Irish Christians had virtually the whole Bible by heart. Inevitably the pupils would differ considerably in natural ability. If Aidan found among his pupils one who was academically gifted (as he did Chad), he sent him over to Ireland to continue his studies at the great Irish monasteries there. At Lindisfarne we don't know the teaching methods used in the school, whether the pupils were taught in groups or individually. No doubt there was much flexibility. A good deal of learning – how to be Christians, monks, priests, missionaries, bishops – would have been learned by apprenticeship and simple imitation, by living alongside men to whom these were the most important things in life.

Where Aidan got his boys for the school we are not told. He was not the sort of man to imprison a child, or to keep him there if he proved unsuitable. Bede mentions that, as the monastery became popular and Aidan began to receive gifts from the rich, the best use he could find for money was to buy children out of a life of slavery. Some of these came and joined the school (EH iii 5). Others no doubt came seeking Christian education, and yet others were perhaps orphans or sent by their families. But they were not necessarily there for life unless they wished it. The story of St Wilfrid shows that it was not difficult for them to leave at the completion of their schooling if they did not choose to be monks at Lindisfarne.

Once the school had been inaugurated and the training of the next generation of leaders had begun, Aidan could turn his attention to the mission to the pagans, his main work.

In that kind of society, where the ruling classes were expected to rule in everything, mission had to begin with the aristocrats. So our first vision of Aidan as missionary is the rather humorous picture given by Bede (EH iii 3) of Aidan addressing a group of no doubt astonished ealdormen and thegns in Irish, while King Oswald (who of course had learned Irish well in his years of exile) stood beside him and translated into English. This would have done the mission no harm: those nobles would have admired the cleverness of their king and also noted how important the Christian faith was to him. The language problem had to be dealt with, for Aidan intended to speak to the ordinary Anglo-Saxons directly. Bede tells us that the bishop was 'not completely' at home in English (EH iii 3). Not completely? Does this suggest that there was some knowledge of English at Iona, perhaps dating from the days of the family of Aethelfrith in exile? Perhaps Aidan had done some preparation before he came? He intended to walk the lanes and speak to the people and of course the king could not accompany him there: kings did not walk anywhere and were always accompanied by nobles. A king's company would have killed Aidan's mission stone dead! So he and his monks had to apply themselves to learning English. We don't know what methods or what aids they used but they seem to have mastered the language.

Out in the mission field Aidan would have made what use he could of the king's facilities. All kings had to be peripatetic, patrolling their kingdom, keeping an eye on their people, particularly the nobles. So they had stopping places such as the one at Yeavering not far from Lindisfarne. No doubt Aidan made some use of these as bases for the different areas he wished to approach. When the king was present and people gathered to one of these bases Aidan could have taken opportunities to speak to groups of them. But the impression we gain is that his main method was to walk the lanes and talk to all the people he met.

To those people there would be two shocking aspects to this. First, that although he was a bishop (and therefore an aristocrat) he was walking. Everyone knew that peasants walked and aristocrats rode horses. King Oswine, one of the kings with whom Aidan became friendly after the death of Oswald, was so perturbed by Aidan's practice of walking that he actually gave him a beautiful horse. But Aidan gave it away to a beggar and continued walking. When the king remonstrated with him (EH iii 4), offering poor quality horses for beggars if required, Aidan replied, 'Surely this son of a mare is not dearer to you than that son of God?' The king eventually agreed that Aidan was right. In these words of Aidan perhaps a reason can be seen for his success as a missionary. In that society beggars were despised: if Aidan could really see in a beggar a potential son of God something of this revolutionary insight must have communicated itself to the beggar and to others. But Aidan did not want a horse. He wanted to be on the same level as the people he was talking to, for he was giving them the completely new idea that God himself had come down to human level, had made himself humble and vulnerable. How could he give that message from the back of a horse?

It was shocking also to the people he met in the lanes that Aidan and his monks travelled unarmed. In that extremely violent society all adults carried knives. But how could Aidan speak of the Gospel of Peace with a dagger stuck in his belt? So, every time the monks went out they risked their lives, and if they were attacked out in the wild the friendship of the king could hardly save them.

When he met people as he walked the lanes, Aidan needed first to establish a starting-point for the conversation. It seems that he asked people about their current religious position. It was necessary to find out where they were, for the situation was complex. If they were English they might be pagans who knew nothing whatever about Christianity, not even the word. But Paulinus, Aethelburh' s chaplain in the days of Edwin, had been working in the area quite recently. So Aidan might meet some who had been converted by him and then either reverted to paganism or managed to remain Christian. The former might consider themselves 'inoculated' against Christianity and be hard to reach; the latter might be happy to meet a new Christian leader. They might even have been converted by Corman, who perhaps was not such a failure as he thought. Aidan tried to encourage people like this in every way that he could. But the people on the road might have been Britons, who had been driven downwards in society by the English conquest but not driven out. With these Aidan would have needed to be very tactful. If they were Christians they could have been Christian long before the Irish, and they might not have liked to be taught their faith by this newcomer who was the puppet of the English king. Or, if they were British pagans, who had chosen against Christianity long before, why should they change their minds now?

We can only suppose that Aidan met some snubs and rejections, and had to have the ability to go on after he had been snubbed and the ability to live with the ever-present possibility of attack and death. Since the impression we are given is that this work was the bulk of his life for 16 years, he must have had nerves of steel.

It would have made good sense for Aidan to organize follow-up visits by his monks to the places where contacts had been made, and Bede, in his tribute to the Irish monks when they left (EH iii 26), is eager to report that these visits were welcomed. The villagers became aware that the Christians never asked for anything for themselves: they were anxious only to give, in preaching, baptizing or visiting the sick. So, says Bede, they were gladly received as God's servants wherever they went. Bede looks at the seventh century a fraction rosily, comparing it with the decadence of his own eighth century, but his impression was that Aidan and his mission succeeded.

The position of women

One further aspect of Aidan's work concerned the position of women in his Christian world. Although double monasteries (monks and nuns in the same establishment under the same head) were to become popular in Anglo-Saxon England, the monastery and school at Lindisfarne remained for males only. A possible reason for this lies in the nature of the mission. Lindisfarne was principally a missionary training college, but public opinion of the time would not have accepted women walking the lanes and accosting strangers as the men missionaries did. It would have been counterproductive, bringing the Christian faith into disrepute, and Aidan did not attempt it. But it is clear that he wanted women to be able to become nuns if they wished and he wanted girls to be able to get education. He encouraged both Heiu and Hild as abbesses (see Chapter 5).

Aidan possibly had two reasons for supporting Religious Life for women. One was that it created an alternative for them, a worthy career for Christian women and a haven for Christian widows. There were many of these. One result of the devotion among upper-class men to the life of warfare and 'glory' was that in that society women normally outlived men. But upper-class widows could be in a very difficult position. A widowed queen would hardly be welcomed by her husband's conqueror in the castle where she had once been mistress. Yet for a widowed queen or other noblewoman to be a nun, or even better to found a monastery and be its abbess, was a congenial and respected solution. So, many of the early nuns were widows. A second reason, in all probability, why Aidan wanted to promote the life of nuns was that books were needed everywhere the Christian faith spread. All books had to be handwritten by someone and educated nuns in their cloister could be vital for this. And if the nun secretly wished to be a missionary she could be comforted by thinking that the books she copied, especially the Gospels, could be seen as themselves carrying the Christian message and so the nun-scribe could see herself as a missionary too.

Aidan's miracles

The miracle tradition connected with Aidan is small. Perhaps a full-scale *Life of Aidan*, had there been one, would have recounted more, for all saints were expected to display the gifts of the Spirit in unusual spiritual powers. Little miracles may lurk almost unnoticed. For example, in Bede's story of King Oswald's Easter dinner at which Aidan was present (EH iii 6) surely the main stress of the story is on the king's charity in giving the whole meal away to beggars and on Aidan's delight that he did so. But Aidan took the king's right hand and said, 'May this hand never perish'. This detail, hardly intended as a miracle, turns into one when Bede mentions that Oswald's arm and hand did not decay and in his day were kept in a silver shrine at Bamburgh. But three stories are recorded specifically because they are miracles.

First, while Aidan was in retreat on the Inner Farne, Penda, the hostile, aggressive but very successful King of Mercia at this time, who stalks like the Big Bad Wolf in and out of the pages of Bede, had come up with his army to Bamburgh and was besieging the king and the townspeople in the little wooden town. He was building a fire around it and, as Aidan could see as he watched all this in horror from the Inner Farne, when that fire was lit the current direction of the wind would carry the flames quickly to the wooden houses and castle. Aidan can do nothing but pray and Bede gives the words of this his only recorded prayer: 'Lord, see what evil Penda is doing!' In the circumstances that was a truly remarkable prayer. A lesser man might have leapt up and down, calling down the curse of God upon his enemies. Aidan asked God to look at it and then do what he willed. The story has a happy ending: the wind changed and the smoke was blown back on the attackers, who abandoned the siege and went home. Aidan was a powerful man of prayer.

Second, when the princess Eanflaed from Kent was to marry King Oswiu, a priest who was to escort her north by sea and was afraid of a possible storm came to Aidan for prayer and reassurance. Aidan told him that there would indeed be a storm; he gave him a little bottle of oil and told him to pour it on to the sea during the storm. He did so and the sea calmed. This story showed both Aidan's gift of prophecy and the power of his blessing in the oil.

The third story concerns a block of wood. Aidan died at Bamburgh, leaning against the outside wall of his little wooden church. The church was burnt down by another attack of Penda but the block of wood against which Aidan had been resting when he died refused to burn. So it was built into the next wooden church on the site. But that also was burnt, this time through carelessness, yet that block of wood refused to burn. So it was placed as a pillar inside the next church and people used to go both to pray beside it and to chip off bits of wood which worked healings. Is this a way of saying that although Aidan was dead his work was indestructible?

Compared with the body of miraculous material connected with Cuthbert (see Chapters 6 and 8), especially the healing stories, this is a very small miracle collection. For many modern people miracle stories cause problems. Probably the right question is, 'What were people anxious to say when they told the miracles stories?' For us, faced with a miracle, the obvious immediate question is, 'What is the truth (meaning the facts) here?'; usually we have no way of answering that, especially when dealing with historical narratives. It is likely that medieval people asked more readily, 'What is meant here? What does this story tell us about God, about the saint, about the situation?' Such stories were often told as the best way of expressing the impact of a particular person on other people and on his/her surroundings. So what was the impact of Aidan that it could best be expressed through these stories?

The comparative thinness of this tradition leads us to ponder on the fact that, although Aidan was the founder of Lindisfarne, as the centuries passed he was eclipsed by Cuthbert, who became the most famous and powerful saint in the north of England. Cuthbert was much more what the early medieval mind looked for in a saint: he had converse with angels, he had second sight and the gift of prophecy, he had the gift of spiritual healing, he became a holy hermit, and finally after death his body did not decay. Further, Cuthbert was English whereas Aidan may always have seemed somewhat foreign.

It is difficult to assess exactly what Aidan achieved. The monastery here remained; other monasteries were founded; missionaries trained at Lindisfarne went to many places in different parts of the country. This led Bishop Lightfoot of Durham in the nineteenth century to the extreme claim: 'Augustine was the Apostle of Kent, but Aidan was the Apostle of England!' This is fun to quote but might be difficult to justify historically.

Interest in Aidan has certainly revived recently. Would it be true that people are now less interested in signs, wonders and the survival of relics, and more interested in human personality and achievement? Aidan was the man who came with great courage and charity to attempt a job another monk had declared impossible. He was a beaver of a man, sticking to the work he had undertaken until either it or he was finished. He worked by getting alongside the ordinary people, learning their language and listening to their experience. We have no records that can judge the effect of such a man's life.

What St Aidan brought

Aidan himself would have maintained that his faith and practice were entirely orthodox, that is what at the time was called 'Catholic' in contrast to any heresy. In his day there was only one Christian church throughout the world, and he would have been appalled at the thought of belonging to any other body or separatist group. Yet the way Christians have worked out their faith and life has always been subject to regional variations and emphases. As Aidan himself wrote nothing, as far as we know, but other Irish Christians wrote a great deal, we need to look at Irish Christianity as a whole to work out some general points in what is called nowadays 'spirituality'.

Perhaps first we may put a confidence in their mission and their message. They did not doubt that they had something supremely worthwhile to give. That the monks went out among pagans to give and not for any other reason is a point which much impressed Bede. Their faith was in God the Trinity and in the Incarnation; they were quite straightforward in this and had no disposition to seek to penetrate God's secrets. Perhaps they were aware that they did not have the sort of mind that enjoys niceties of doctrine and philosophy. But they had a very strong belief in God as present and active. Without that they could not have gone out into the world as adventurously as they did. In particular, *peregrinatio* could not have caught on without a very vivid sense of the guiding, accompanying presence of God.

God is known, then, not through argument but through obedience. How is his will known? Through the truths revealed in the Scriptures. Of all the branches of Christian theology the Irish liked biblical studies best. They studied the Bible not to worry about deeper meanings when the plain truth eluded them, but to ask the question, 'How does God want us to live?' and to seek an answer in the holy text. When they felt they had found one they went out and lived like that. Simplistic? But immensely effective, as they found when they went on to the continent of Europe.

The Irish had not been literate before they were Christian and literacy came to them in its Latin form. Every book belonging to their new religion was in Latin. They did not find it an easy language but they tackled it with great enthusiasm and success. To them the purpose of all Christian study, and the height of all Christian intellectual endeavour, was to be able to understand and interpret the Scriptures, because that was the way God made himself known. Where, then, the will of God was clear there could be no argument. They would never have understood a version of the Christian faith without prayer, without fasting and alms-giving, without an attempt to forgive enemies. All was obedience, and if death came in the course of obedience, so be it!

Spiritual helps were available in the form of angels, who could take many shapes. There were also spiritual enemies, the Devil and demons, who tried to ruin human relationship with God. But in the Irish tradition, unlike the Desert Fathers for example, there is surprisingly little about demons. A person's main enemy, in the struggle to live the life of obedience, is him/herself, his/her own laziness and love of comfort. These things must be overcome by discipline, by a strong asceticism. Yet, in dealing with the failings of others, the Irish monks appear very compassionate. They had a worked-out system of ritual medicine for all sins and some of this was tough, but they insisted that there is no such thing as a sin which cannot be dealt with. So never despair!

Their life had a goal, sufficiently described in the Scriptures: the life of heaven, the Kingdom of God, the Final Consummation of God's will, the Second Creation. As a second creation this would put right all that had gone wrong with the first; it would restore harmonies that had been lost. One of those harmonies had been between man and the animals (Genesis 3) and of this restoration they occasionally saw signs even in this present age; hence the number of lovely stories of friendships between saints and wild animals. So they lived in hope, looking forward to a glorious fulfilment in the future. Of course men who thought like that had a great deal to give, and with that background Aidan and his monks came to Lindisfarne to begin to give it.

'St Aidan's Prayer for Holy Island'

The following prayer was in the possession of Marygate House on the Island when I first came 30 years ago. St Aidan did not write it, but we don't know who did. I include it because it seems to me to contain so much of the spirit of the first monastery. It has sometimes been quoted, or even misquoted, in other printed material, but this is the text as it was given to me:

> Lord, this bare island, make it thy place of peace.
> Here be the peace of men who do thy will.
> Here be the peace of brothers serving men.
> Here be the peace of holy rules' obeying.

33

Here be the peace of praise by dark and day.
Be this thy island, thy holy island.
Lord, I, thy servant Aidan, speak this prayer.
Be it thy care.

4

St Aidan's Boys

The founding of the school on Lindisfarne was probably the most enduring thing that Aidan did. He seems to have been good at choosing suitable boys, and of course as the years went by many more were educated in the school than those whose names we know. We are reminded of this invisible host when occasionally, in the pages of Bede, we meet for the first time others who, we are told at that point, were trained on Lindisfarne, such as Diuma, an Irishman who later became the bishop of the Middle Angles and Mercians, and Adda and Betti who went with Diuma and Cedd on the Middle Anglian mission.

This chapter deals with the careers of the best-known: Eata; Cedd, Chad and their brothers Caelin and Cynebill (whom we assume to have been at the Island school); and the young Wilfrid. It does not deal with Cuthbert except in so far as Cuthbert's early life was so closely connected with Eata when they were both at Melrose. Cuthbert was never a pupil in the school here. The sense in which Cuthbert might be included as a 'St Aidan's boy' must depend on our interpretation of that incident when, aged 16 or 17, he was guarding some sheep on one of the local hills and saw in the night a vision of angels escorting a human soul to heaven. That was the night when Aidan died, and it was the turning-point in young Cuthbert's life, leading him to seek a monastery. Perhaps we may look at this from Aidan's angle and say that the last act of this saint who had influenced so many young people, on his last journey from earth to heaven, was to reach out a 'hand' and touch a boy!

Eata

Of the first 12 boys in St Aidan's school Eata is the only one who can be named with certainty. The others whose names we know may have come a little later. Eata must have been an older teenager when he came, as by St Aidan's death in 651 he was already Abbot of Melrose. At this time the minimum canonical age for ordination as a priest was 30 years (though we do know of abbots who were not priests). But presumably to take older teenagers at the beginning would have suited Aidan's plan for a trained English leadership for the English church as soon as possible, given the uncertainties of life for the Irish in a foreign country.

The monastery of Melrose, founded by Aidan, was not on the site of the present town but about two miles east. The site, called 'Old Melrose', is now part of farmland and there is no public access to it. The seventh century buildings were destroyed in 839 by the Scottish leader Kenneth McAlpin. It has been the best known of Aidan's other foundations.

Little is known about Eata's personality. Bede calls him 'the gentlest and simplest of men'. He was abbot when Cuthbert requested permission to enter Melrose although, since he was away at the time, the decision to accept Cuthbert was taken by the prior, Boisil, and Eata ratified it on his return.

Eata clearly was the sort of leader who accepted a challenge. Alhfrith, son of King Oswiu, had been made sub-king of Deira by his father. He offered Eata 40 hides of land at Ripon to found a new monastery there. (A hide was sufficient land to support a family; it differed in size according to the fertility of the land, but this was a generous offer.) Eata, with a group of his monks including Cuthbert, founded this monastery, where for a time Cuthbert was guest master. But Alhfrith developed anti-Irish pro-continental views, perhaps as a result of his friendship with Wilfrid. The Melrose monks were given the chance to change their opinions but they refused. They returned to Melrose and Ripon was given to Wilfrid.

It is difficult to get a chronology for the next bit of the story. Plague (probably bubonic) at Melrose carried off among others Boisil the prior. Cuthbert was then asked to become the next prior. The following two or three years saw him as an active missionary in the area. But then, when all the Irish monks and some English left Lindisfarne following the decision of the Synod of Whitby (see Chapter 7), Eata was asked by the king, at the suggestion of the departing Irish bishop, Colman, to become Abbot of Lindisfarne also. He agreed, but sent his prior, Cuthbert, into residence at Lindisfarne; to what extend Eata himself lived on the island is not recorded. The Lindisfarne monastery at that point consisted of those English monks who were prepared to accept the decision of the Synod, or who were unconvinced but not prepared to emigrate. Of course they were in some disarray: they had just lost all the senior members of their community. To bring them into order was something of a challenge, which Cuthbert had to meet.

So for the next few years Eata was Abbot of Melrose and Lindisfarne. The next bishop after the departure of Colman was Tuda, probably chosen because he had been educated in the southern part of Ireland, where the problems that arose at the Synod of Whitby had been faced and solved a few decades earlier. No doubt it was felt that he would be a reconciling influence. But unfortunately he caught the plague immediately afterwards and died. Wilfrid was then chosen to be bishop and moved his centre from Lindisfarne to York. After some years Wilfrid was expelled from Northumbria after a quarrel with King Ecgfrith, son of Oswiu, who had succeeded his father in 670. It must have been apparent to everyone (except Wilfrid, who never accepted it) that the northern diocese was far too big for one bishop, since it covered virtually the northern half of England. Wilfrid's enforced absence allowed the reforming Archbishop of Canterbury, Theodore of Tarsus, to divide up the diocese. At first it was simply split into its two natural parts, Bernicia and Deira, and Eata returns to the story as Bishop of Bernicia with his centre at Hexham or Lindisfarne. To this work he was consecrated at York by Archbishop Theodore. But then a further division was seen to be necessary. Eata remained at Lindisfarne as its fifth bishop while a certain Tunberht was appointed to Hexham.

But three years later the Archbishop deposed Tunberht. The unwilling Cuthbert, by this time a hermit on the Inner Farne, was elected bishop without his permission. He was expected to go to Hexham but refused. Then Eata asked Cuthbert to go to Melrose for a 'conversation', at which it seems that Eata offered to transfer to Hexham himself, so that Cuthbert could be Bishop of Lindisfarne, which Cuthbert accepted. If this is a true interpretation of these rather confused events it shows something of Eata' s character: that he was the sort of man who seeks for a solution in a difficulty and is prepared to implement it even at some cost to himself.

Eata died shortly after these events, in 685 or 686. He was followed as Bishop of Hexham by John of Beverley, who had been trained by St Hild at Whitby and so had a more remote link with Aidan through her.

Cedd

Bede tells us (EH iii 23) of four brothers, all of whom became priests and two of whom went on to become bishops. The assumption is that they were all trained at Lindisfarne. Bede names them as Cedd, Cynebill, Caelin and Chad. This may well have been the order of their age: some of Cedd's actions suggest he was the eldest.

Cedd's first work as a missionary was among the Middle Angles, a people whose land covered modern Leicestershire, Northamptonshire and neighbouring areas. They were under the overlordship of King Penda of Mercia, who had placed his son Peada over them as sub-king. Peada wished to marry Alhflaed, daughter of King Oswiu of Northumbria. (Royal relationships are rather fascinating: Oswiu's son Alhfrith was already married to Penda's daughter. But royal marriages did not

imply royal family affection. Penda had already killed Oswald
and was himself to be killed by Oswiu.) Oswiu required Peada
to accept the Christian faith before he married his daughter. So
Peada came north, was instructed in the faith, and was so taken
with it that he said he would accept it even if he could not marry
the girl. Then he was baptized by Bishop Finan, who had succeeded Aidan, presumably was married, and asked for missionaries to accompany him to his country and instruct his people.
Four were chosen: Cedd, Adda, Betti and Diuma.

But after a while Cedd was withdrawn from this mission by
King Oswiu (note the power of the king!) and, with another
priest, sent to the East Saxons. Oswiu had just succeeded in per-
suading Sigeberht, King of the East Saxons and a friend of his, to
accept the Christian faith and be baptized. Naturally both kings
then wanted missionaries to go to evangelize the people of Essex.
Cedd appears to have been particularly successful. He came
home to consult Bishop Finan who then, with two other bishops,
consecrated him as Bishop of the East Saxons. He returned south
and promoted a very fruitful mission, founding churches, ordain-
ing clergy, preaching, baptizing and founding, according to Bede
(EH iii 22), two main centres at Bradwell-on-Sea and at Tilbury.

But Bede's next story shows a different side to Cedd's character, which can be paralleled in the lives of other Irish or Irish-
trained saints. Cedd had excommunicated a nobleman who was
'unlawfully married' and had forbidden anyone to communicate
with him. But the king, presumably quite unused to any interfer-
ence with his relationships with his nobles, had gone to visit him.
Cedd was furious and pronounced that the king would meet his
death in that same house at the hands of the same man and his
brother, which did in fact happen. Bede regrets his death, for he
was in every other way an ideal Christian monarch. But Cedd
here was behaving like any Irish saint, who showed no defer-
ence to nobility where Christian faith or morals were concerned.
Even the gentle Aidan could show great firmness according to
Bede (EH iii 5), who writes about him: 'Neither respect nor fear
made him keep silent about the sins of the rich . . .'

Even though Cedd's main work was in Essex he did not forget his native Northumbria. On one of his frequent visits home his brother Caelin, now a priest and apparently a kind of chaplain to Oswald's son Oethelwald, now sub-king of Deira, introduced him to this king. Oethelwald invited Cedd to found a new monastery on land he would donate, where he could come to pray and where he might be buried. He asked Cedd to choose the site which, according to Bede (EH iii 23), was very wild, fit for robbers and wild beasts rather than humans (although in fact it was not too far out in the wilds, being quite near a Roman road). As already mentioned (Chapter 3), Cedd first, to cleanse the site of spiritual evil, embarked on a 40-day Lenten fast: every evening he would eat a little bread, one hen's egg and a small drink of milk and water. But ten days before the end of the fast the king summoned him. So Cedd called on his other brother Cynebill, who was also a priest, to complete the fast for him. Then the monastery of Lastingham was built and the monastic programme of Lindisfarne was adopted there. It is an interesting feature of this story that the 40-day fast was objective: it did not have to be a spiritual feat of Cedd himself. It was thought of as a battle against spiritual evil, and it did not matter who was the warrior as long as the right side won!

When the Synod of Whitby was called by King Oswiu (Chapter 7), Cedd was invited to attend as interpreter. He presumably was fluent in English, Irish and Latin. An interpreter was needed because of the variety in the membership of the Synod. King Oswiu spoke English and Irish but not Latin; the Irish monks present might have had some doubts about their English; one of the bishops present, Agilbert, who was a Frank by origin although at this time was Bishop of the West Saxons, thought that Wilfrid would be a better speaker of English than himself. An interpreter was needed who could make sure that all present understood the proceedings: he must be thought trustworthy by all sides. It seems that Cedd did this very competently.

But the year of the Synod, 664, was also a very bad year for the plague. We believe this to have been bubonic plague, like the later Black Death and the Great Plague of London. This plague was endemic at the time, but certain years experienced particularly bad outbreaks. Cedd, having accepted the decision of the Synod, on his way back to Essex happened to call in at his monastery at Lastingham. There he caught the plague and died. His last act was to make his brother, Chad, Abbot of Lastingham. When news of his death reached Essex, 30 monks from one of his monasteries there came north to be near his body but sadly, with the exception of one small boy, they all caught the plague and died.

Cedd appears once more in the story. Years later, when Cedd's brother Chad had been a successful and much beloved bishop in Mercia, he too was warned of his coming death by plague. The warning consisted of a visitation of angels and spiritual beings, including Cedd, accompanied by beautiful music. Chad died a week later as he expected. Interestingly, Bede tells that a certain Egbert, an English monk living in voluntary spiritual exile in Ireland, who had known Chad in his younger days, reported that in Ireland he had had a vision of Chad's brother Cedd descending from the sky with angels, and returning to heaven taking Chad's soul with him. Cedd was the responsible elder brother right to the end!

Cynebill and Caelin

These two brothers of Cedd and Chad, both priests, are mentioned only in the story of the foundation of Lastingham.

Chad

We first hear of Chad when, with his brothers, he joined Aidan's monastery on Lindisfarne and again later, when he was a youth in Ireland living the monastic life and studying the Scriptures. The explanation for his time in Ireland may be that Aidan, seeing that Chad was academically able and eager for study, sent him there for further education. Bede tells us that many

English youngsters went to Ireland either to study or to live a more ascetic life. Some became monks; others preferred to travel around, learning all they could from one monastery and then moving on to another. The Irish monks were extremely kind and hospitable to these foreign students. They gave them their daily food, their books and their tuition, all free (EH iii 27). The two Irish specialities which attracted attention at this time were Biblical studies and asceticism.

We do not know how many years Chad spent in Ireland, but he had returned in time to become Abbot of Lastingham on Cedd's death in 664. A story of his time there as abbot shows something of his character. One day a man turned up at the door of Lastingham wearing plain working-man's clothes and carrying an axe and an adze. He explained that he wished to be a monk but to concentrate on manual labour rather than on reading, writing and Latin. He was in fact a man with a distinguished career behind him, named Owine. He had been head of the household to Queen Aethelthryth when she came from East Anglia to marry King Ecgfrith. But she really wished to be a nun and persuaded the king eventually to release her. Owine then decided to become a monk and wherever possible, when the other brothers were reading, to work outside. It is a tribute to Chad's openness of mind that he accepted such an unusual and in a sense perverse novice.

The next bit of Chad's life-story is difficult to understand fully. After the Synod of Whitby and after the death of Tuda, Wilfrid had been chosen as bishop. He preferred to have his centre not at Lindisfarne but at York. But he did not wish to be consecrated as bishop in England: he preferred to make sure that it was done 'properly' in Gaul. So it was, in a gorgeous ceremony which he must have enjoyed greatly. But then he lingered in Gaul, remaining after his consecration for too long a time for King Oswiu, who wanted a working bishop. So Oswiu decided that Chad should become Bishop of York instead, and sent him to the kingdom of the West Saxons, to be consecrated by Bishop Wine (who was later to be accused of simony) and two British bishops. Chad was humble enough to accept this consecration but later it would cause trouble. Why he was prepared to take on a diocese which he must have known had been given to another is something of a mystery: most likely he was moved by the spectacle of the people without a pastor. Chad then worked as a bishop very much in the tradition of Aidan and Lindisfarne, travelling on foot not horseback, preaching the gospel, visiting over a wide area.

Then Wilfrid returned. The problem was left to Theodore of Tarsus, Archbishop of Canterbury, to solve. He restored Wilfrid, explaining to Chad that his consecration had not been acceptable. (This was because he had been consecrated by British bishops, whose validity was doubted by the church on the continent.) Chad's reply, 'I never thought myself worthy of it', so impressed Theodore that he re-consecrated Chad himself. He kept him in mind and although Chad humbly withdrew to Lastingham Theodore persuaded him to come out of retirement and become Bishop of the Mercians and of the people of Lindsey. Chad established the centre of his see at Lichfield and for two years was a very busy bishop there. But Theodore was doubtful about Chad's custom of walking everywhere. He ordered him to ride whenever he had a long journey and, when Chad seemed hesitant, 'the archbishop lifted him on to the horse with his own hands' (EH iv 3).

A story told of Chad at this time (EH iv 3) shows something of his spirituality. His monks noticed that at the first sign of a high wind or a coming storm Chad would lay aside his reading, or whatever he was doing, and begin to pray. If the storm got worse he would prostrate himself in prayer. If it turned into a really powerful thunderstorm Chad would go into the church and pray devotedly until the storm was over. When asked why he did this Chad explained that it was a God-given opportunity, because of the threatening nature of the storm, to meditate on our sins and the real threat of the Last Judgment or of some more immediate act of God's power. So he used the storm to practise self-examination and to pray for God's mercy upon the human race.

Among the monks who had come with him to Lichfield from Lastingham was Owine. When Chad received warning of his death, by an angelic visitation accompanied by beautiful music, the rest of the monks were inside, reading, but Owine was outside, digging. Chad was alone in his little oratory at the time; he called Owine and asked him to summon the monks. He told them that he had had a forewarning of his own death. When they had gone away sorrowful, Owine asked about the heavenly music, which only he and Chad had heard. So Chad confided in him what he had not told the others, that he would die in exactly one week's time, as he did.

Of all Aidan's disciples Chad seems to have been the nearest to him in character and methods.

Wilfrid

One more 'boy' must be mentioned, who was very different. For Wilfrid we are not dependent solely on Bede; there is a remarkable other source. One of Wilfrid's monks who was very close to him, Eddius Stephanus, sometimes called 'Stephen of Ripon', wrote a *Life of Wilfrid* very soon after his death. It is the nearest thing we have to a contemporary life, but it is still hagiography not biography, and is complicated by the fact that the writer had an extravagant devotion to his subject.

Only the first part of Wilfrid's life concerns us here. He was born in 634 or 635, which makes him an exact contemporary of St Cuthbert. He was a nobleman's son and presumably received the military training appropriate to his class. But at about 14 years old he decided to leave home, partly to pursue the idea of a religious life and partly to escape the cruelty of his stepmother. His father equipped him as a young nobleman and he went to the court of King Oswiu. Here he formed a friendship with Queen Eanflaed and confided his hopes to her. She arranged for him to become the attendant of a nobleman called Cudda who, partly through physical infirmity, wished to live the monastic life on Lindisfarne. So Wilfrid came to the Island two or three years before the death of Aidan; he saw that there was a school and presumably asked permission to receive education; he learned to read, write and to understand Latin, none of which was a normal part of the education of a nobleman's son. Wilfrid was clever and impressed Cudda and the other monks. But at the age of 18 he decided not to become a monk on Lindisfarne. He wanted if possible to go to Rome. Queen Eanflaed continued to help him by arranging for him to stay with her kinsman the King of Kent, and from there, accompanied initially by another young noble, Benedict Biscop, who was later to become the founder of Wearmouth/Jarrow, he left for the continent.

For Wilfrid that journey to Europe and eventually to Rome was the decisive experience of his whole life. They travelled first to the city of Lyons where Wilfrid decided to stay for a time while Benedict went on. At Lyons the Archbishop, Annemundus, was so attracted by Wilfrid that he was prepared to organize for him a career in local government, to give him a niece in marriage and to adopt him as his son and heir. But Wilfrid, though grateful for the friendship and promising to renew it, went on to Rome.

There he fell in love with everything Roman. He daily visited all the shrines and made another important friendship, with Boniface the archdeacon, who recognized the young man's intellectual gifts and taught him a good deal of Roman customs and canon law. Boniface organized an audience for him with the Pope, who gave him his blessing. So Wilfrid left Rome, carrying a good number of relics, and travelled back to Annemundus. He stayed there for a further three years, continued to study and at that point became a monk. He very nearly became a martyr also, for Annemundus was in fact embroiled in conflict and killed. Wilfrid returned to Northumbria, made friends with Oswiu's son Alhfrith and was given the site of Ripon, from which Eata and the Melrose monks were expelled.

When Wilfrid was in Rome, with its impressive buildings, wonderful past, inspiring shrines and other religious sites, its orderly church life and learned people, we must suppose that the little wooden huts of Lindisfarne seemed to him so primitive, so restricting that he returned almost as a missionary to the Irish monks, to give to them and to his own Northumbrians something of the wonders he had seen.

His opportunity was coming. He will re-enter the story of Holy Island at a slightly later date.

5

The Abbesses

There was no girls' department in Aidan's school on Lindisfarne
and no resident women in his monastery, though nothing, as far
as we know, prevented women from visiting him there. But the
influence of both Aidan and Lindisfarne went far beyond the
Island itself. Bede writes of two women who were trained by
Aidan for the Religious Life, and then of two more who came
well within his 'orbit'.

Heiu

The first is the mysterious Heiu. Bede tells us that she 'is said'
to have been the first nun in Northumbria and that she was
'ordained by Bishop Aidan' (EH iv 23). She was the first Abbess
of Hartlepool but we are given no date or mention of the other
nuns there. Soon after founding that monastery, for some unknown reason, she moved to Tadcaster and nothing more is
known about her. But this brief mention is evidence that Aidan
was anxious actively to promote the Religious Life for women.
The monastery at Hartlepool was eventually inherited by Hild,
with whom Aidan had much more success.

Hild

Hild was born in 614 into a family which was soon to become
the foremost in Northumbria. Her father Hereric was a nephew
of Edwin, who within two years of Hild's birth would become

king. Her mother was Breguswith and she had one elder sister, Hereswith. Hild's name means 'battle' and the form she would have known was 'Hild', not 'Hilda', which is the Latin form used by Bede.

It is doubtful if Hild ever knew her father. At the time of her birth the kingdom was still ruled by the hostile King Aethelfrith (see Chapter 1), until he was killed in battle in 616. Edwin himself at the time of Hild' s birth was a refugee in exile, and so was Hild's father, who was living at the court of Ceretic, King of the British kingdom of Elmet. Hereric died there and the rumour was that he was poisoned.

Bede tells us (EH iv 23) of a dream Hild's mother had at this time which was a prophecy of her baby Hild's life and importance. She dreamed that she was searching for her husband and could not find him, but in her garments she found a most precious necklace which glowed with so much light it filled the whole country. There are a number of stories of this kind, in which the mother of some important person has a dream, either during pregnancy or at the birth, of a glorious future for the child. The original readers would have picked up the meaning without worrying about the 'truth' of the story.

Hild was probably brought up at her great-uncle's court. Since Edwin was of the royal house of Deira, the southern part of Northumbria, it may be that her childhood was spent largely in York. Until she was 11 the English of Northumbria were pagan in religion, but then King Edwin married Aethelburh, daughter of Aethelbert of Kent, the king who had welcomed Augustine and his company to Canterbury. The new queen was Christian; the marriage treaty guaranteed her freedom, the right of her chaplain to evangelize, and the King's own serious consideration of the Christian faith. Two years later Edwin was baptized at York by the queen's chaplain, Paulinus, and among those baptized with him was 13-year-old Hild.

Then we lose sight of her. At the age of 13 she was considered to be old enough to marry. Royal ladies were much in demand to cement alliances between families and kingdoms. Did she marry? In fact we don't know, because it seems that Bede didn't know. When he knows that a lady was not married and became a nun he calls her 'a holy virgin'. When he knows that a lady was married and then became a nun he calls her 'a holy matron'. He simply calls Hild 'God's holy servant'. There could have been a short-lived marriage we know nothing about. Many aristocratic marriages were short-lived because of the fondness of aristocratic men for killing each other on the battlefield, so there were many widows, and women usually outlived men.

But perhaps, even at the age of 13, Hild had a sense of a different vocation with which marriage was not compatible. Perhaps she 'battled' to be allowed to fulfil it. We don't know. But certainly at some point she began to be educated in a way royal ladies usually were not: reading, writing, the Bible, other Christian writings. By her mature years she was a very learned woman.

When she was 19, wherever she was living at the time, King Edwin was killed in battle and the life of the court went into chaos. The queen with her young children fled back to Kent; with her went the bishop Paulinus. If Hild still lived at home perhaps she went too. Soon in Northumbria there was a new Christian king, Oswald, and a new missionary bishop, Aidan, and a new Christian centre, Lindisfarne. But we do not hear of Hild again until she was 33 years old, the date was 647, and she had decided that she wished to be a nun.

Meanwhile her elder sister, Hereswith, had married into the royal house of East Anglia, had been widowed and now herself was a nun at the monastery of Chelles in Frankish Gaul. Bede explains that as there were not yet many monasteries in England a number of monastic aspirants had gone over to Gaul, including a number of English girls. He mentions Chelles as one of the places that attracted these ladies (EH iii 8). Hild decided to join her sister at Chelles.

So she left wherever she was and went first to the royal court of East Anglia. There were three good reasons for this. First, it was a good embarkation point for Gaul. Second, as the sister of

Hereswith she would have been welcomed there as a member of the family. Third, this remarkable family was passionate about promoting the monastic life. The King of East Anglia, when Hild arrived, was named Anna. In the future three of his daughters, a step-daughter, a grand-daughter and a great-grand-daughter would all become founders and/or abbesses of monasteries. In that family Hild would not have lacked encouragement to pursue her vocation.

How Aidan knew about her, and how he knew her whereabouts, we do not know. He wanted to promote the Religious Life for women (see Chapter 3) and somehow, either by going in search of her in person or by sending a powerful message, he persuaded Hild to abandon her plans and return to Northumbria. This decision might have involved a considerable sacrifice for her. She had been going to her sister but also, by going abroad, she was giving up her native land. So she would have had the sense of being a *peregrina* (see Chapter 2), one who abandons everything for God, which she might have desired. However, she did return; Aidan established her, with a few companions, on a small site on the north side of the River Wear with just one hide of land, sufficient for a single family. He and others trained her in monastic ways and then moved her, presumably with her companions, to Heiu's site at Hartlepool. Eight years later Hild moved south to found the great Abbey of Whitby. We have no record of her having visited Lindisfarne, though in view of its importance as the mother monastery it seems very unlikely that she did not come here at some point.

Both Hartlepool and Whitby were 'double monasteries', that is, monks and nuns in the same establishment. These appear to have originated in Gaul and then spread to England where, for a time, although there continued to be monasteries for men only, all the houses for women were double. Theories have been suggested to explain this: since women could not be priests they would have needed men to celebrate Mass and the sacraments; and since they could not do hard physical work they would have needed men for the tough jobs, especially if the monastery had lands and a farm. In England, though not in Gaul, all the double houses we know of were under the rule of an abbess, never an abbot. We must imagine that monks and nuns lived in separate accommodation, though all the details of the life would have been decided by the abbess since written Rules were not yet universal. As already mentioned, there would have been many royal and noble widows and the abbesses were drawn from that class. When the Greek monk Theodore of Tarsus came to be Archbishop of Canterbury he was worried by the double monasteries but decided not to interfere with local custom. They gradually died out over the next centuries.

But during the time that Whitby flourished under the Abbess Hild, it was, says Bede, important as a place for training the young. The learned abbess seems to have been also Principal of her school. She compelled her students to give part of their time to Bible studies and part to the performance of good works (EH iv 23). Bede mentions five who became bishops and a sixth who was appointed a bishop but died before he was consecrated. Presumably there were many others trained at Whitby, including nuns, whose service to the church at this time was invaluable.

But if we ask what kind of person Hild was, perhaps the best answer comes from the story we have from Bede of Caedmon (EH iv 24). He was a cowherd on the monastery's land at Whitby. He was probably a Christian and quite illiterate, but he had a further problem: when the farm labourers all met in the evenings to have dinner together they would entertain each other by passing round a little harp and each chanting a song or poem. For some reason which is not made clear poor Caedmon could not do that so, feeling lonely, miserable and inadequate he retired to the cowshed. One night he had a vision or dream. It seemed to him that a heavenly presence stood there and gave him the power to make songs and sing them. In particular the visitant commanded him to sing about the Creation and so, in the dream, he did. When he woke up the dream proved true. He could remember the songs and sing them. So he told his immediate boss, the farm bailiff, and together they went to tell the abbess. Hild, with some senior monks, listened to him seriously but asked him to undergo a test: they would tell him a Bible story of their choice and he would come back by the next day with that story made into a song. He did. Hild wasted no time: she invited him to become a brother in the monastery, not in order to learn Latin, but to make into English poems and songs the Biblical material they would recount to him. He was to help the ordinary people to know, remember and enjoy the Bible. So he did for many years. His poetry has not survived to our age; still, he is the earliest English Christian poet and we owe him to Hild.

For this story is not simply about Caedmon. It reveals the character of the abbess. Society was clearly divided into classes and she was of royal blood and advanced education. Yet she was open-minded enough, humble enough, to accept that God might have given to a mere cowherd a gift that neither she nor her monks and nuns had received. We might expect that an Anglo-Saxon noblewoman would be able to exercise power. But to be able to enable other people, as she enabled Caedmon, goes beyond any ordinary exercise of power.

Bede tells us that she had such good sense, such wisdom, that not only ordinary people but also kings and princes wore a path to her door to share their difficulties and receive her counsel. He says that she had great energy and great industry. He does not tell us what part if any she played at the Synod of Whitby (see Chapter 7). This was held in her monastery during the time she was abbess, but it was the king's meeting: was she even allowed to be present? As it happens there is another source in addition to Bede. A monk of Ripon, Eddius Stephanus, a friend and disciple of Wilfrid who wrote the *Life of Wilfrid* shortly after his death, has a little in that book about the Synod and says clearly that Hild's sympathies were on the Irish side and that she was hostile to Wilfrid. She would have been a powerful enemy. She even sent embassies to the Pope to counter the claims Wilfrid was making at Rome. Yet Eddius Stephanus, for all that he was devoted to Wilfrid, was sufficiently impressed by Hild to refer to her as 'the holy mother and pious nun Hild' and to imply that she was in fact present at the Synod.

She lived to the age of 66 but had a distressing illness over the last six years. On the night of her death at Whitby, says Bede, a nun called Begu, inmate of Whitby's daughter monastery at Hackness, woke to hear the Whitby convent bells some miles away and to see the roof open and a great light pouring in. Looking hard at the light she saw in it the soul of Hild being borne to heaven. She woke all the other nuns there to prayer for the rest of the night. But daybreak brought some of the Whitby monks with the news that it was indeed true (EH iv 23). Hild had died on 17 November 680. It was the same year, though probably not the same day, that a little boy of seven was handed in by his guardians to the monastery at Wearmouth. His name was Bede.

The opinion of the great Anglo-Saxon historian, Sir Frank Stenton, is often quoted: 'No woman in the Middle Ages ever held a position comparable with that of Hild of Whitby.' We may ask why not? We can see that Hild was lucky (or should we say it was providential?); lucky in her birth into the most powerful Northumbrian family of the time; lucky in her outstanding qualities of personality and intellect; lucky in her contact with Aidan and other church leaders. Should we say that her time of birth in the early seventh century was also lucky/providential? Were there external factors in society which mattered? The historian Patrick Wormald thinks so. He points out that this time, the period of first- and second-generation Christianity among the Anglo-Saxons, shows many aristocratic women founding monasteries and becoming members of them. I have mentioned already the royal family of East Anglia, but in Kent and Wessex the ladies were equally active. The same was happening across the sea among the Franks. What was enabling all this?

Patrick Wormald is clear that the double monasteries were, in essence, nunneries. This is shown by the fact that they were ruled (in England without exception) by abbesses. The men were important, whether they were priests serving the community, students moving up to ordination, simply monks living their chosen way of life, or essential labourers on the estate – all these were important, but the nuns were dominant. But, he says, there were conditions in society which enabled these women to flourish at this exact time, as they could not later on.

First, it was a 'heroic' culture. Aristocratic males were trained to fight and nothing else. So to these soldiers the world of monastic and literate culture might be fascinating but a little bit 'unmanly'. A king' s son would not normally go to a monastic school. King Aldfrith, son of Oswiu (see Chapter 10), could become a scholar only because he was not expected to come to the throne. But women of the upper classes were free of all that. They did not fight but they could exercise Christian leadership. It was a time of rapid change; the new faith was excitingly experimental; there was scope for them.

Second, property was an important issue. In this society women could possess and keep their own property, which might be inherited from their parents or might be a bridal gift from their husbands as was customary. Women lived longer than men (because the men died in battle) and women could accumulate wealth, which made them desirable to men looking for rich wives. But if they used that wealth to found a monastery and to become a member there it meant that their property remained with them and with the original family, not subject to a second marriage. This was an important consideration.

Third, women were reckoned to have a certain psychic power which gave them a superiority in religious matters. They could be the spiritual wing of the family and pray for its spiritual needs. This was an appropriate women's role. If they became nuns they were 'brides of Christ' and brought their kinsmen into a particular relationship with God.

How did it all change? For even by the middle of the eighth century it was changing. Wormald's opinion is that the men were more committed to traditional ways and took to Christianity more easily after it became less experimental, more established. Then they took it over. The scope for women's leadership narrowed. Documents show us that fewer nunneries were founded. Charters giving women property rights became gradually scarcer. Even the correspondence of a man like Boniface, who wrote over several decades, shows a gradually decreasing proportion of letters to women. New monastic foundations were largely for men. The scene is being set in every way for the 'High Middle Ages'.

So St Hild was lucky: she did live at the right time.

Aebbe (Ebbe)

Aebbe is usually thought of as the second Northumbrian woman saint, after Hild. She was the daughter of Aethelfrith and sister of Oswald and Oswiu. The records are too sparse for us to reconstruct all her life-story. It is possible that, as a child, she accompanied her brothers into exile on the west coast of Scotland and there met the monks of Iona and was taught and converted, as her brothers were. Certainly at some point she met and embraced the Christian faith. We do not know her age and it is therefore possible that, while her brothers were in exile, she was already married and living elsewhere, as Anglo-Saxon girls married very young. It has been conjectured that she married into the royal house of Wessex, but this is based mainly on the existence of an old parish dedicated to St Ebbe in Oxford, which was within the area of Wessex. However, there are at least two other St Aebbes, one connected with Repton and one with Thanet, both a little nearer to Oxford than is Northumbria. We simply don't know where she spent her married life.

As a widow Aebbe returned to Northumbria with the intention of becoming a nun. Being a king's daughter she would naturally think of founding a monastery herself. A later source says that her brother Oswiu gave her a site at Ebchester for her first monastery. Then she moved to Coldingham, which is now north of the Scottish Border but then was in Anglian Northumbria. There the site for her monastery was an old Roman fort on the cliffs above the sea and in this bleak and beautiful place she spent the rest of her life.

Coldingham was a double monastery like Hartlepool and Whitby. There are a number of stories about it. The first tells of a visit by Cuthbert while he was still a member of the Melrose monastery (see Chapter 6). Abbess Aebbe invited him to come and talk to her community; of course he joined in the daily worship while he was there; but one of the monks noticed that he left the monastery after evening prayers. He decided to follow Cuthbert to spy on him. Cuthbert went down to the sea and spent the night praying and singing psalms, in and out of the water. At daybreak he came up on to the beach and with him came two sea-otters, playing around him and warming him with their hot breath. Cuthbert blessed them and they went back into the sea, while he turned to go up to the monastery. Then the spy-monk came out from behind his rock and flung himself down before Cuthbert, terrified.

The saint understood what had happened and said he would forgive the monk provided he did not tell anyone what he had seen until after his, Cuthbert's, death. The monk promised, but Bede says he more than made up for it after Cuthbert was dead (VA ii 3; VP x).

Obviously there is more to this story than that of a man who had a gift with wild animals. The clue is in the terror of the spy. He would have been soaked in the Bible stories, so he would have known that at Creation humans and animals were in harmony (Genesis Chapter 2) which was then broken by man's sin (Genesis Chapter 3). But he would have read also the prophets' hope that one day God will restore the harmonies, the 'lion shall lie down with the lamb' and God will bring in his new creation. The monk would have read in the New Testament of the coming of God's Kingdom, one day. But it was believed that where there is a saint, who is nearer to God than most people are, God's Kingdom can begin to operate in advance of the great day of its final coming. That monk would have seen, on the beach that morning, not a man playing with a couple of otters but Christ in his saint restoring the harmonies of his creation. He would have felt that he had been spying, impertinently, sacrilegiously, on the Kingdom of God. No wonder he felt terrified.

A second story about Coldingham does not end so happily. In that house was a certain Irish monk named Adamnan. Bede says he was so austere that he ate and drank only on Sundays and Thursdays and often spent whole nights in prayer (EH iv 23). One night Adamnan had a vision: a heavenly being stood by him and congratulated him on his vigils and prayers and then revealed that no one else in the monastery was occupied in that way. Either they were asleep, or they were feasting, drinking, gossiping or (the nuns) occupied in the latest fashions. So, said the visitant, this monastery will be destroyed by fire.

Adamnan confided in another monk, who made sure Abbess Aebbe heard about it. When she had the details from Adamnan she tightened up the discipline there for a time, but after she died the lax behaviour began again, and the monastery was burnt down.

Bede does not like reporting scandal and this is the only one of the double monasteries of which this kind of story is told. It may not seem very serious to us, but given the importance of the monastic life to them it was serious indeed. It might create the impression that Aebbe was not a very competent abbess. Yet everyone spoke well of her. The third story shows her exercising some personal and political power.

King Ecgfrith, Oswiu's son, was of course Aebbe's nephew. He had been married at a young age to Aethelthryth, whose first husband, an East Anglian nobleman, had died. But she wished above all to become a nun; she had preserved her virginity through her first marriage and intended to do the same in her second. Obviously this did not please Ecgfrith, who wanted both a normal marriage and an heir. Aethelthryth looked up to Wilfrid as a counsellor and so the king asked him to persuade her to consummate the marriage. Instead he supported her in her desire to be a nun and the king eventually allowed her to go. She went to Coldingham for a year and presumably was trained under Aebbe; then she returned to East Anglia, where she founded the monastery at Ely.

So Ecgfrith married again, quite legally, as he was entitled to do. But it left a dislike of Wilfrid; the new queen, Iurminburg, was suspicious of Wilfrid's great power (as also were most of the kings). The next part of the story is told by Eddius Stephanus, Wilfrid's friend. Wilfrid had just returned from Rome, where he had persuaded the Pope to rule that the whole northern diocese, which had been subdivided by Archbishop Theodore, should be returned to him. So he brought back the papal decree and a large number of relics. But King Ecgfrith and the Northumbrian nobles simply laughed at him and put him in prison. It seems that the queen took the relics-box and wore it as a kind of necklace. But then Ecgfrith and Iurminburg went up to Coldingham to see his aunt the abbess and there the queen became seriously ill. Aebbe then intervened and told Ecgfrith that the queen would not recover until he either restored or at least released Wilfrid. The king could not bear to restore him to his earlier position as bishop of the whole kingdom but he did release him and restore his relics, and Wilfrid went into exile. The queen recovered and Eddius was full of praise for Aebbe.

The abbess then fades out of the story. She died in about the year 683.

It is not possible to say whether she ever met Aidan, but she could not have lived in Northumbria during the seventh century without being under the influence of Lindisfarne.

The stories about her help to build up the whole picture of the environment in which our first monastery and its people lived and worked.

Aelfflaed (Alflad or Elfled)

Aelfflaed entered the Religious Life even younger than Bede, as a baby of one year. The circumstances were these: she was the daughter of King Oswiu and Queen Eanflaed. Her mother, when she was a new-born baby and the first child of King Edwin and

Queen Aethelburh of Kent (see Chapter 1), had been baptized by her mother's chaplain, Paulinus, as a thanks-offering for her father's escape that day from a murderous attack. After Edwin's death in battle Aethelburh and her family went back to Kent. Eanflaed was brought up there and at the age of 16 returned to Northumbria to marry Oswiu.

Their child, Aelfflaed, was born in 654 so never knew Aidan, who died in 651. But since she was handed over to Hild at Hartlepool and lived all the rest of her life in that community, moving with them when Hild founded Whitby, she would have heard all the stories about Aidan. No doubt the regime in the monastery would have been basically that established by Aidan.

Baby Aelfflaed's father Oswiu, who seems to have been less of a fighter than his brother Oswald, had been faced with a massive threat from the heathen King Penda of Mercia, who was just victorious from the battle where Oswald had been killed. Oswiu attempted to buy Penda off with a gift of treasure, and it seems that Penda and his army had turned away southwards when Oswiu attacked. Although the Mercians had a much bigger force it seems that Penda was taken by surprise; his troops were defeated and he was killed.

Before the battle Oswiu had made a double vow to God: if he were victorious he would dedicate his baby daughter to the Religious Life and would give 12 estates of ten hides each (sufficient for ten families) for the foundation of new monasteries. Two of the monasteries to benefit from this were Coldingham and Whitby.

So Aelfflaed was given into the care of Hild at Hartlepool and moved with her to Whitby when it was founded two years later. There she grew up and was groomed eventually to succeed Hild as abbess. When King Oswiu died of natural causes in 670, the only one of the seventh-century kings of Northumbria to die in his bed, his widow Eanflaed became a nun at Whitby, and when Hild died in 680 Eanflaed and Aelfflaed ruled Whitby as joint abbesses for a time, presumably until Eanflaed's death, the date of which is not known; thereafter Aelfflaed was sole abbess.

Aelfflaed was a close friend of Cuthbert. Three stories illustrate this. On one occasion she persuaded him to meet her on Coquet Island, which at the time had its own community of monks and was an obvious midway point between Lindisfarne and Whitby. She arrived with some of her nuns and he with some monks. She had three pressing questions: how long would her brother King Ecgfrith live? Who would succeed him as king? Would Cuthbert himself become a bishop? The answers, put into rather mysterious language, were: Ecgfrith would live for one more year (so this meeting must have been in 684); he would be succeeded by his and her half-brother Aldfrith (then in exile in Ireland); yes, Cuthbert would become a bishop if asked, as he could not think of any way to avoid it (AV iii 6; VP 24)!

On another occasion both Cuthbert and Aelfflaed were at 'an estate belonging to her monastery'. At the time Cuthbert was a bishop and engaged in a final visitation to some of his diocese, as he had a premonition of his death and wished to retire to his hermitage. So the year must have been 686. During their meal together Cuthbert suddenly stopped eating, turned white and dropped his knife. On being questioned by Aelfflaed he explained that he had just 'seen' the soul of a man from her own monastery being taken to heaven, but did not know his name. Aelfflaed naturally sent a messenger posthaste to Whitby; all the monks there were alive and well, but investigation showed that one of the shepherds, having some reason to climb a tree, had fallen out of it and died. Aelfflaed received this news in time to interrupt Cuthbert's Mass next day to ask him to remember this man, whose name was Hadwald (VA iv 10; VP 34).

The third story relates that when Aelfflaed herself was ill and could not be cured of the persistent weakness following the illness, she suddenly thought that if only she had something belonging to Cuthbert (Bede says she said 'my Cuthbert') she would be fully cured. Then, astonishingly, a gift from Cuthbert arrived, a girdle. Aelfflaed put this on and in the next two days was completely healed. The girdle worked its healing power also on a nun in that community who had severe headaches, which ceased when it was bound round her head. This girdle mysteriously disappeared. Bede thinks that was to prevent any misuse of it by anyone who was not worthy (VP 23).

These stories are told mainly to demonstrate Cuthbert's heavenly powers: the gift of second sight, the gift of prophecy, the gift of spiritual healing. They show him also as capable of personal friendship, even with a woman, though of course a woman dedicated to the same way of life as his own. As for Aelfflaed, they show her as the caring mother of her community. In relation to Cuthbert she is the good, but dependent woman.

Did Bede in fact 'tame' his abbesses? The question might arise when we consider that he would hardly have known any real women, as he entered the monastery at the age of seven and very rarely came out. He would have known from his biblical studies about really bad women, such as Queens Jezebel and Athaliah, and many really good women, of whom the Virgin would have been in every way the first. We might suspect that he thought of really good women as essentially receptive, a foil to good men. But to answer the question we need sources other than Bede for purposes of comparison. For Hild we have no other major source. But for Aelfflaed there are two other sources: the anonymous *Life of Cuthbert* (see Chapter 6 for details) and Eddius Stephanus' *Life of Wilfrid*. A comparison between the way Aelfflaed is presented in Bede and in the anonymous *Life*, for example in the stories just mentioned, gives the impression that Bede had made Aelfflaed far more of the 'silly woman' than she was, just by altering a few details, in order to exalt his hero. Eddius writes very warmly of Aelfflaed. When he is trying to record a peace-making process between King Aldfrith (Aelfflaed's half-brother) and Wilfrid he mentions two letters from Archbishop Theodore, one to the king and one to the abbess urging her to promote peace. Clearly he thought of her as having political influence. Later he refers to her as the 'most prudent virgin' and 'always the comforter and best counsellor of the whole province'. Eddius shows her included in the membership of a synod where she spoke up on behalf of Wilfrid, bearing witness that King Aldfrith before he died had wished that Wilfrid should be re-instated and had left instructions to his son to do this. She is represented at this council as being consulted by the Archbishop himself (*Life of Wilfrid* ix).

Eddius is favourable to anyone who is on the side of his hero Wilfrid, but his book does indicate, as Bede does not, a more public and political role for the abbess, for which she had the necessary gifts of strength and wisdom.

She died at the age of 59 in the year 713.

6

After Aidan

Aidan died at Bamburgh on 31 August 651 and was buried at Lindisfarne. It is clear that the monastery at Iona still considered itself to be in charge of the Northumbrian mission as it then consecrated and sent Finan, presumably one of its own monks, of aristocratic Irish stock, to be the second bishop. He was Bishop of Lindisfarne for ten years; on his death Iona sent the third bishop, Colman, who returned three years later after the Synod of Whitby (see Chapter 7). The time of Finan and Colman coincided with St Cuthbert's early years after he entered the monastery at Melrose. During the years covered by this chapter Oswiu, brother of Oswald, was king over the whole of Northumbria.

Finan, Bishop of Lindisfarne 651–61

During Finan's time as bishop the Christian mission from Lindisfarne expanded, partly as the boys trained in the school grew up and partly as King Oswiu himself undertook the conversion of at least two other kings and took an interest in the evangelization of their kingdoms.

Two episodes in particular show the growth of the mission. The first has already been mentioned (Chapter 4). It concerns Peada, who came to marry Alhflaed, Oswiu's daughter, and accepted the Christian faith. He and his company were baptized by Bishop Finan at a royal estate known to Bede as *Ad Murum*, which Bede describes as 'close to the wall which the Romans once built across the Island of Britain' and 'about 12 miles from the east coast'. Among the priests whom Peada then took home with him was one Irishman, Diuma, who later was consecrated by Bishop Finan as 'Bishop of the Middle Angles and the Mercians' since there was a shortage of bishops at the time. After his death another Irishman, Ceollach, followed him in this position but after a short time resigned and went back to Iona. These are fascinating hints of a continuing flow of people between Iona and Lindisfarne during these years. Of course there were also Irish in the other kingdoms who had no connection with Iona and Lindisfarne.

King Oswiu then persuaded his friend King Sigeberht of the East Saxons to become Christian. Then Oswiu, presumably with Bishop Finan's approval, withdrew Cedd from the Middle Angles and sent him, with another priest, to be head of the East Saxon mission. When this gave evidence of success Finan, with two other bishops perhaps from the Ionan connection, consecrated Cedd as the first bishop of the East Saxons. It is interesting that Cedd, although he was working so far south, still considered himself part of the northern mission and did not liaise with the Christians based at Canterbury.

Bede records (EH iii 25) that here on the Island Bishop Finan built a church, presumably a second church to Aidan's original. It was obviously a finer building 'suitable for an episcopal see'. It was built in the Irish style, of hewn oak thatched with reeds; later, on a visit to the north, Archbishop Theodore of Tarsus dedicated it to St Peter. This is the church in which the remains of St Aidan (eventually) and of St Cuthbert were interred. It is thought that it was within the area of the Island now enclosed by the ruined church of the later monastery. An archaeological dowser who visited the island found the foundations of a large rectangular building within this space but of course it has not been possible to excavate.

Bede records one further incident about Finan (EH iii 25). He was passionately attached to the convictions held at Iona about the date of Easter. This was a very divisive matter (see Chapter 7). For some reason he was visited by another Irishman, Ronan, who was passionately (indeed violently, says Bede) convinced of the rightness of the continental position. A major row occurred. Bede says that one of the two was 'a man of fierce temper' but it is not clear which one! Nothing was solved at this time, however, but the incident prepares for what is to come.

Then, after ten years on Lindisfarne, Finan fades out of the picture. But he could have died well satisfied with his years here, which had seen the strong development of the mission, still in very close contact with the mother monastery on Iona. He was followed by Colman.

Colman, third Bishop of Lindisfarne 661–4

Colman also came from Iona, but his episcopate lasted only three years during which the only recorded incident is the Synod of Whitby (see Chapter 7).

But after the Synod, when the Irish monks decided to leave Lindisfarne, we must not necessarily suppose that they 'stomped out'. It seems that right from the beginning Aidan had expected English church leaders to take over: that was why he trained English boys. Of course the Irish monks had to leave at this point. The first rule in politics at the time was that no one in a kingdom was more powerful than the king. The king had chosen against them; both they and anyone who could not or would not accept the King's decision had to leave the kingdom. But the evidence is not that they left in anger. As for the 30 English monks who chose to go with Colman, there could have been a number of reasons. Some might have been genuinely attached to Ionan customs, and others genuinely attached to their Ionan leaders. Some might have learned from their Irish teachers about *peregrinatio* (see Chapter 2) and have seen a chance to put this form of asceticism into practice by voluntarily leaving their native land.

Colman took with him some of the bones of St Aidan as relics, and they departed.

The sequel, however, is bitter-sweet. First Colman took his

Irish and English companions to Iona, but they could not stay there permanently. So he looked for a site for a new monastery, initially for both groups together. He found a place on the island of Inishbofin, just off the west coast of Ireland. But differences of temperament, or differences in farming practice (or whatever) between the two groups surfaced: in the spring the Irish monks departed while the English monks cultivated the land. At harvest the Irish monks returned, but the English monks were not willing for them to share the fruits of their toil. Eventually Colman decided another new monastery was needed and found a site on the near mainland at Mayo, which a friendly chief was prepared to let him have on condition that the monks prayed for him. There Colman settled the English monks, leaving the Irish on Inishbofin. In Bede's time Mayo, which became known as Mayo of the Saxons, was still staffed by English monks. So Colman also fades from our story.

Bede's tribute to the Irish monks of Lindisfarne (EH iii 26)

At this point, the departure of Colman, Bede inserts into his narrative a generous tribute to the Irish monks, concerning whom it seems that he admired everything except their calculations of the date of Easter. Their buildings on Lindisfarne, he says, were minimal, just the bare necessities for the life of the community. They had cattle but no money. If anyone gave them money they promptly gave it away to the poor. If they were visited by wealthy people, including the king himself with a handful of his thegns, it was assumed that these people came to pray; if they stayed for a meal they ate whatever the brothers were eating, nothing else and nothing more. Bede is glad to note that the monks were well respected by the ordinary people, indeed they were popular. If a cleric or a monk visited a village the people were glad to be blessed by him or to hear his message. The people knew that the monks never came to ask for anything for themselves, but only pastorally to give, that is, to preach, to baptize, to visit the sick. The monks resisted efforts by the wealthy to give them lands or possessions, even in order to found monasteries, unless this was clearly essential in the eyes of the secular authorities too.

All this Bede admired. His general outlook was that the seventh century was a time of genuine faith, whereas his own century, the eighth, showed decline from such high religious standards.

Cuthbert's early years

At first sight there seem to be four sources of information about Cuthbert, which would be wealth indeed. Then we realize that these are not four separate sources: three of them were written by Bede and he was heavily dependent on the fourth.

These sources are, first, a *Life of Cuthbert* written by an anonymous monk of Lindisfarne about the year 705. Bede drew on this when he wrote his own books, but it is good that this anonymous work also has survived. No doubt it contains many first-hand memories of Cuthbert; it includes some material that Bede did not include and it approaches some of the stories differently. (This book is indicated here by the letters VA.) Second, a verse *Life of Cuthbert* written by Bede, but now hardly used except by experts because it is in difficult Latin and not easily available; the suggestion is that Bede wrote it for monks who practised slow and meditative reading. Third, Bede's prose *Life of Cuthbert*, written at the request of Bede's friend Bishop Eadfrith and the Lindisfarne monks. Bede, who rarely left his monastery, actually came to Lindisfarne to research this, and it became the 'authorized' account. (The letters VP indicate it.) Fourth, some chapters in Bede's *Ecclesiastical History* which set the life of the saint in a wider context.

So we follow the story according to Bede. Cuthbert was born in the year 634 or 635, at the time when Aidan was founding the monastery at Lindisfarne. We know nothing about his parents and it used to be the fashion, especially in children's books, to present him as a 'shepherd-boy', that is a peasant. This has been queried for several reasons, all of which suggest he came from a well-to-do family.

For example, he had a foster-mother, Kenswith, of whom he was very fond. He must also have had a foster-father who trained him to fight, if the anonymous *Life* is right in saying that he was in at least one battle. Fighting was an upper-class occupation; boys went on to the battle field for the first time at about 14 years old. Fosterage itself was an upper-class system; it was very sensible in a violent age where children might need the protection of an alternative family. It often worked well, with strong bonds of affection between foster-parents and children and between foster-siblings. It did not mean that the natural parents did not care for the child. We don't know, however, anything about the circumstances in which Cuthbert was fostered.

Some stories of his youth indicate a 'good' background. When, as a child, he had a bad knee he was carried to sit outside by 'the servants' (VP ii). As a youth he rode a horse. There is only one story that connects him at all with sheep (VP iv) when, guarding someone else's flock of sheep and so staying awake in the night, he saw angels come down from heaven and escort a human soul back there. (This proved to be the night when Aidan died.) But guarding the sheep, presumably against the Border Rievers of the time, was a perfectly appropriate action for a well-born young warrior. In later life he mixed easily with kings, queens, abbots and abbesses, which might have been difficult in that society if he had been of peasant stock.

There are legends about his childhood which show him already as a leader. Legends do not necessarily contain 'historical truth', but they always show the thinking of the people who told and retold the legends. The story that Cuthbert, as a child of apparently about eight years old, wore out all his little friends in competitions in somersaults and cartwheels, and then was approached by a smaller child who begged him, as a future bishop, to give up this undignified play (VP i), at least shows that people thought of him as marked out for Christian leadership at an early age. A few years later he was among a hostile crowd watching rafts of monks being carried out to sea by a sudden current (VP iii). He alone was prepared to pray for the monks, but his prayer was answered and they got back safely. People who told this story could not believe that Cuthbert was not endowed with spiritual power from an early age.

He emerges into history after the vision of St Aidan's soul when he requested permission to enter the monastery at Melrose. He rode up to the gate on a horse, carrying a spear, both of which he gave to a servant to take home (VP vi). This was no peasant, but why Melrose? It was possibly close to his home; it had been founded by Aidan as a daughter house of Lindisfarne, perhaps on the site of an earlier British settlement, since the name *Mail Ros* is British; it had a prior, Boisil, probably an Irishman judging by his name, who had a great local reputation as a saint and a teacher. The Abbot of Melrose at this time was Eata, but he was not in the monastery when Cuthbert arrived. So Boisil accepted him and Eata afterwards ratified this decision.

Cuthbert was a keen and devoted novice, diligent in the spiritual life of the monastery and in reading and working. The hardest thing for him was the fasting (taken seriously in an Irish monastery), but after all he was only about 17 years old and very strong and energetic in body.

When Eata was given land at Ripon for a new foundation Cuthbert went with him as part of the founding party and there he was made guest master. This was an important position. A guest was to be treated as if he were Christ himself, and so the guest master must always be warm and welcoming. From later material it seems that Cuthbert was indeed an even-tempered, sunny, sociable man. But one story that is told about him at this time (VP vii) indicated not his personal qualities but his growing reputation for spiritual gifts, including converse with angels. It was winter; snow had fallen; a man came to the guesthouse; Cuthbert greeted him and went to get food at the bakehouse. But on his return there was no guest; there were freshly baked loaves from somewhere, with a wonderful scent; there was only one door but when Cuthbert looked out there were no departing footsteps in the snow. An angel!

But the days of the Melrose monks at Ripon were numbered.

They had been given the land by Alhfrith, son of Oswiu. But as he became aware of growing problems of differences within the Christian community, especially between the Iona-based Irish party and the Christians from Kent who were much more in touch with the continent of Europe, he moved away from the Irish outlook. His mother Eanflaed, although she was Edwin's daughter and had been born in Northumbria, after her father's death in battle had been taken as a small child to Kent, the kingdom of her mother's family. So from childhood she was used to continental customs. When Wilfrid returned from the continent where he had spent some years he wanted to give some of the gorgeousness of Roman Christianity to his own people. He and Alhfrith became friends and then it occurred to Alhfrith that Wilfrid would be a much more suitable Abbot for Ripon than the Melrose monks. So Eata and his monks were expelled. They returned to Melrose and Ripon was given to Wilfrid.

But a tragedy hit Melrose, probably the worst thing that could happen to a close group of people: plague. Cuthbert caught it but survived, though with a lifelong weakness which caused him internal pain. His friend and teacher Boisil also caught the plague and was to die of it. Bede tells the story (VP viii) of how Boisil, correctly predicting that he had seven more days to live, suggested to Cuthbert that they should study St John's Gospel together, which he had in a convenient copy in seven sections. So they read and discussed one section each day and on the seventh day, after having prophesied that Cuthbert would become a bishop, Boisil died. He had been prior of the monastery; the Abbot, Eata, now asked Cuthbert to become his next prior.

At this point in his life Cuthbert did some of his major work as an evangelist. He travelled from Melrose up into the hills, looking for people who had not yet heard the Christian message, going to places 'which others dreaded to visit' says Bede (VP ix). Sometimes he stayed away on these preaching tours for as much as a month. He was apparently a skilful and persuasive teacher. One of the best-known incidents occurs at this point, already described in Chapter 5: how, when visiting his friend the Abbess

Aebbe of Coldingham, he spent the night on the beach and was warmed the next morning by the breath of two sea-otters.

He began to develop the spiritual gifts which, in the minds of people of the time, marked out the saint: gifts of prophecy, experiences of the ministry of animals in meeting his needs, experiences of detecting and driving out demons, of changing the wind through his prayers. Many people at this time would have begun to be aware of his unusual gifts and to predict for him an unusual future.

After the Synod of Whitby and the departure from Lindisfarne of the combined Irish/English party, Abbot Eata found himself also Abbot of Lindisfarne. He transferred Cuthbert to the Island, to have a position of authority and teaching here. So the next stage of Cuthbert's life began.

7

The Synod of Whitby

Leading up to the Synod

The Synod of Whitby proved to be a turning-point in the story of Holy Island in that it brought to an end the presence on the Island of the Irish monks from Iona, who had come so courageously to set up the first monastery, the school and the missionary work. The Synod was a meeting called by King Oswiu in 664 to find solutions for some of the problems of the Church which had arisen because of the differences in practice between the Irish monks based on Iona and continental Christianity, with its main centre, in this country, at Canterbury.

Whitby was chosen as the site for the Synod probably for two reasons: it was a royal monastery since the land for its foundation had been given by Oswiu himself, so he felt a degree of possessiveness towards it; and being on the coast Whitby was easy of access, an important consideration in that age when people found sea travel easier than the forested and largely road-less mainland. At the time of the Synod St Hild was Abbess of Whitby, but that might have been irrelevant: we do not know whether she was present at the proceedings or not. One of our sources implies that she was there, but Bede does not mention her. We know that her sympathies were on the Irish side. Those present were the King in the Chair; for the Irish, Colman and some of the Lindisfarne monks; for the 'Romans' a Frankish bishop, Agilbert, currently bishop of the West Saxons, Wilfrid, the aged James, the deacon who had remained after the earlier mission of Paulinus, and others.

There are two sources for the Synod's proceedings: Eddius Stephanus' *Life of Wilfrid* (Chapter 10) and Bede's *Ecclesiastical History* (iii 25). Bede's is by far the longer account. But both accounts are slanted to the Roman side. Here it is important to remember that neither writer is a 'historian' in our sense. Their accounts of the Synod are incorporated into their total message, that is, Eddius writes for the honour of his hero Wilfrid and Bede for the honour of the united Church. There was a further convention concerning the writing of speeches, which Bede may have known and used. From the days of the Greek historians it had been acceptable for a narrator, when describing a speech, to put into it his own ideas of what was fitting to be said on the occasion, since he had no first-hand knowledge of what was actually said. St Luke uses this convention in the writing of Acts, and Bede may well have understood and accepted it.

So we should not treat even Bede's description as minutes of the meeting! Wilfrid in reality might not have been as rude about the Lindisfarne monks, who had first educated him, as he appears.

Other important personages in the story were the queen, Eanflaed, and Oswiu's eldest legitimate son, Alhfrith. We have met them both already in Chapter 4. Eanflaed, daughter of King Edwin, had been baptized here by Paulinus, but when Edwin was killed her mother returned home to Kent. So Eanflaed was educated in the south, in the continental, not the Irish, tradition of Christianity. She seems to have kept to continental customs when she came back north to marry King Oswiu. One consequence of this concerned the date of Easter (see below): differences here would mean that sometimes the king would be feasting and celebrating Easter while the queen was still fasting and keeping Lent. No doubt, in those days when people both fasted and feasted very vigorously, this could have been a minor embarrassment, but probably it should not be over-emphasized. The king and queen did not live side by side in a peasant's hut.

The king's halls were spacious and the king and queen often had different roles to perform.

Possibly the main promoter of the idea of a synod was King Oswiu's son Alhfrith. He had been made sub-king of the southern part of Northumbria, Deira. It was common for a king to allow his eldest son to take over part of the kingdom in this way. But Bernicia and Deira were in a very fragile union. The kings of the family of Aethelfrith belonged to Bernicia, but King Edwin and therefore his daughter Eanflaed were originally from Deira. Possibly Oswiu hoped to unite the two parts more closely by marrying a Deiran. But Oswiu, who at first was King of Bernicia only, had then organized the murder of his cousin King Oswine of Deira in order to take both kingdoms for himself. In penance for this act Eanflaed had persuaded Oswiu to found the monastery of Gilling. The whole situation was volatile.

So the suggestion is that Alhfrith, sub-king of Deira, wishing to get rid of his father and take Bernicia also, had agitated for a synod to be called. He expected that his father would continue to support the Irish side, would be shown by that to be old-fashioned and out of date, would be more easily disposed of, so that Alhfrith could take the throne. But if he did calculate like this (and we are not sure that he did) his father was too clever for him. Oswiu, to everyone's surprise, declared for the continental side, and it is Alhfrith, not Oswiu, who quietly slides out of history.

We should not think, however, that these political motives were the only ones. There was genuine religious conviction also. Alhfrith had become great friends with Wilfrid and absorbed his outlook: Wilfrid had returned from his continental experience convinced of the rightness of Rome in all things. As for Oswiu, when he declared at the end of the meeting that he would not oppose St Peter who was the keeper of the gate of heaven, he may well have felt quite sincerely that he would be in need of friends at that point. But Eddius Stephanus says he gave his decision 'with a smile' or even 'smiling into his beard'. It is possible that this smile had an element of malicious satisfaction in it.

So the hidden agenda at the Synod of Whitby may have been relationships within the royal family. The explicit agenda dealt with three points: how to calculate the date of Easter; what sort of monastic tonsure was proper; some details about the administration of baptism. The most important item was the problem of the date of Easter. Many modern people may dismiss this as a triviality. It was not, and it will repay a fairly lengthy effort to understand it.

The date of Easter

It would have been an impossible idea to Christians at this time that the date of Easter could be decided merely by matters of human convenience. Easter was the principal feast of the year, much more important than Christmas, which had a fixed date. On the date of Easter depended all the other movable feasts (the beginning of Lent, 40 days before; Ascension, 40 days after; Pentecost, 50 days after). Christians in the early Middle Ages believed that God had chosen carefully the time and place for the Incarnation of his Son, and that he had over many centuries prepared his people for it. God had chosen also the date and place of his Son's Passion and Resurrection. In the early centuries they did not separate the Passion on Good Friday from the Resurrection on Easter Sunday: one single feast (from Holy Saturday into Easter Sunday) celebrated both. The Passion and the Resurrection was the most important event which could ever happen in this world, 'the point where time crossed with eternity' (B. Ward). So God had left instructions for the proper annual commemoration of this supreme moment.

First the Christians looked in the Old Testament for information about the Passover, since Jesus died at Passover time. The regulations for the Passover by itself were clear enough (Exodus Chapter 12). This feast probably originated in those shadowy beginnings of the Hebrew people, long before Abraham, when they were nomads with flocks and herds. In the spring, when their animals had just had their young and they were about to move to their summer pastures, they needed the brilliant light of the first full moon of spring. So they had a ceremony to bring themselves good fortune.

But then, one particular year after Abraham, Isaac and Jacob, when they had become an enslaved people down in Egypt, things changed dramatically; they believed that God had brought them out of slavery and that he chose the Passover night to do it. Passover no longer meant moving flocks: Passover now meant freedom. It was to this miraculous deliverance from slavery in Egypt that they looked back as they celebrated year by year. But by the time of Jesus they were again an oppressed people, under the rule of Rome, so when they celebrated Passover they prayed for a future liberation to match that of the past.

All that is clear enough, and in Biblical times it was easy to calculate the date of Passover, the first full-moon of spring, by simply watching the sky. In the first month of spring count 14 nights from the night when the new moon first becomes visible. That will give the full-moon, and Passover was just a single feast on the night of the full-moon itself.

However, when, after the Exodus, the Hebrews had come into the land of Canaan and settled down, they became arable farmers, no longer just nomads. They continued to keep the Passover, but added to it another feast, the seven-day Feast of Unleavened Bread. This also, like Passover, was a spring festival, but suitable for arable farmers, in that it symbolized the clearing away of the old crops and making space for the new. The two festivals were put together, but unfortunately different parts of the Old Testament differed slightly in details. Deuteronomy began the seven days on the same day as the Passover (Deuteronomy 16) but Leviticus began the seven days one day later (Leviticus 23). This was to add to the problems of the early Christians.

In the New Testament the Gospel texts were easier to manage. All the evidence was that Jesus had died on a Friday and had risen on a Sunday, all during the Passover season. One of the early decisions of the church was that the Christian Feast of Easter should always be on a Sunday. (Passover, of course, could be on any day of the week.) So all Christians could agree on the formula, which is the one we still use: Easter is the first Sunday after the first full-moon after the spring equinox.

Then the problems began. Unlike the Jews, the Christians could not wait until they could actually see the beginning of the Easter moon. They had to know the date of Easter in advance, so that they could begin Lent. So the mathematicians of the early Church set out to construct tables, which would put together the timetable of the sun, to give the equinox, and the timetable of the moon. It was a very difficult mathematical problem, made harder by the fact that the sun's year is not exactly 365 days in length, nor is the moon's month exactly 28 days. However, mathematical tables were produced . . . but several of them. They did not always agree. At the time of the Synod of Whitby part of the problem was that the Irish and the 'Romans' (continentals) were using different tables.

The problems which arose may be put in terms of four questions, to all of which the Irish and the Romans gave different answers.

First, when is the spring equinox? The Romans correctly chose 21 March; the Irish 25 March. So if 21 March was the equinox, and if the next day was a full moon, and if the following day was a Sunday, to the Romans that day would be Easter. (This actually happened in 2008.) But the Irish would wait another month for the next moon, because they said the equinox had not happened and since Easter was the Feast of the victory of light over darkness – very important symbolism to them – it could not reasonably be celebrated while the night was still a little longer than the day.

Second, when does a day begin? The Irish began each day at sunrise. So if the full moon rose at any point during the night of Saturday/Sunday it followed that that Sunday was 'after' the full moon and was therefore Easter Sunday. The Romans began the day in the evening, so any moon rising that night would be part of the same day and they would have to wait a week to get the first Sunday 'after' the full moon.

Third, since the Jewish Passover could occur on any day of the week it would sometimes happen on a Sunday. Was that Sunday the Christian Easter? The continental Christians said 'no': they could not keep Easter on the same day as the Jews kept the Passover. This was not simply dislike of the Jews. Many places on the continent had substantial Jewish populations; there the Christians found it essential to emphasize those things which made them different from Jewish people, especially in order not to confuse the pagans whom they hoped to convert. But there were no Jews in Ireland and the Irish simply did not see the problem. After all, they said, the Jews do not keep Easter, so what does it matter to the Christians what the Jews do? So, if the Passover and Easter would have coincided, continental Christians preferred to wait a week until the next Sunday and keep that as Easter. This worried the Irish as they believed the regulations (following Deuteronomy) laid down that Easter should be between the 14th and the 20th day of the moon. To wait until the 21st day of the moon, or later, would mean that the moon would be visible for less that half of the night. But the symbolism of Easter is light over darkness, so how could they celebrate a 'dark Easter'?

Fourth, is it essential that all Christians agree on this matter? The Romans said 'yes', since increasingly to them it was a question of the solidarity of the Church in doctrine and in custom, and a question of showing a united front to new converts. The Irish hesitated. They would have preferred the rest of the world to agree with them. They were strongly attached to their ancestral practice. Above all, they wished to be obedient to God and to discover and live by his will. This was the major point in their spirituality, and no question of human convenience would have allowed them to abandon it.

Other matters on the Synod's agenda

At the Synod there were two other matters in dispute. One was the practice of baptism, but here we are not sure exactly what the problem was. Both sides would have baptized using water and the formula 'In the Name of the Father and of the Son and of the Holy Spirit', since that is Biblical. Perhaps it was to do with the number of immersions, three or one; in fact we don't know.

The other dispute was about the monastic tonsure. The continental monks left a fringe of hair round their head and shaved the crown. They claimed that this tonsure had a Christian meaning and it became known as the 'crown of thorns' tonsure. The Irish monks shaved the front of the head, perhaps allowing just a fringe at the very front, and let their hair grow long at the back. The continentals objected that this was a pagan Irish practice, a sign of the 'druids'. There could have been truth in this, but the Irish monks presumably felt that it was recognized in their society as the badge of a religious leader and they had no objection to it.

Understanding the participants

We can try to appreciate the motivation of the two sides in the argument. The Irish wanted above all to be loyal to their Christian ancestors, those heroes of faith who had established the new religion and the monastic movement in Ireland. Their position can be understood better through the earliest writings that have come down to us from the pen of an Irish Christian writer, the monk and *peregrinus* Columbanus. He has no sense of inferiority to the continentals. Indeed, after more than 20 years of living in Gaul and Italy he can say that he has been disappointed with continental Christianity: he saw real heroic Christian living back in Ireland and expected to see even more when he came to Europe, but instead he had found a certain passive flabbiness, as if the Christian battle were already over. In the references in his letters to the Easter question he wants, initially, the whole world to recognize that the Irish were right; but later he hopes at least that the Irish abroad will be allowed to keep to their ancestral ways. Probably Colman and the Irish Lindisfarne monks thought the same. Columba of Iona, their founder, was a very powerful saint, living and working now from heaven. How could they turn their backs on what they had been taught and on what had inspired them?

But to the continentals the Irish of Iona were just a small group perched on a fringe of the world. How could they maintain that they were right against the rest of the Church? The decisive point was that the continental side included Rome. Rome was the place of the tombs of Peter and Paul; the Pope was the successor of Peter; Peter was the one who, according to the Gospels, held the keys of the Kingdom of Heaven. The Lindisfarne monks, as representatives of Iona, could cite John, the apostle of whom they were very fond, but in the end it was Peter who had the power.

So King Oswiu decided for the continental side. For Lindisfarne and its story the immediate result was the departure of the Iona monks. No more Irish faces and Irish voices! But it was not by any means the end of Irish influence. The English 'Northern Saints' were all either taught by or inspired by the Irish, and that teaching continued for centuries. Nor is there any reason to suppose that the Iona monks left in high dudgeon. King Oswiu, Bede says, still had a great regard for Bishop Colman, and was able to implement his suggestion that Eata, Abbot of Melrose, should look after Lindisfarne. It was good of Colman to suggest Eata for, if he had been angry, he could easily have looked on him as a traitor since he had been educated on Lindisfarne. Clearly Colman could accept that there were two sides. Perhaps he thought back to the early days of Aidan who, in choosing to educate English boys for church leadership, obviously did not think that the Irish monks were there for ever. But it would have been impossible to stay in Oswiu's kingdom and remain in disagreement with the king. Kings had to be allowed the final voice. So Eata, Cuthbert, Hild, Aebbe, Cedd, Chad and others swallowed any feelings they might have had and accepted the new arrangements. Perhaps Iona felt a little deprived at the loss of one of its satellites and at the fact that it could no longer choose the next bishop of the Northumbrians, but the

Synod was not the end of good relationships between Iona and Lindisfarne.

The 'myth' of the Synod of Whitby

A remarkably enduring 'myth' has arisen about the Synod of Whitby, namely that it was a contest between the 'Celts', wonderfully creative, and the 'Romans', remarkably authoritarian and hidebound. It was nothing of the sort. The Irish of Iona were not representative of 'Celts' (they would have been unaware of both the word and the concept). On the matters at issue, especially the date of Easter, most of the Irish had already taken the same view as the continentals: the southern Irish had 'gone over to Rome' on this matter in 633. They were just as 'Celtic' as the Irish of Iona. Only Iona and its empire of monasteries stood out against the continentals, who were not hidebound but were seeking a solution to a difficult problem, preferably a solution on which the whole church could agree. They had a greater sense than the Irish of the need for the whole Christian community to move together against the heretic and the pagan because, after all, the continentals lived in a wider world.

The problem occurs when the Synod is hijacked and forced to serve the interests of later disputes: Protestant against Catholic, Irish against English, 'Celt' against the rest. So the result of the Synod has been presented as a tragedy, an incomparable loss to Northern English Christianity. But it was not a tragedy in any sense. Probably the result was historically inevitable. For Britain, though not Ireland, had been part of the Roman Empire and so had many traditions of earlier contacts with the continent, and the Anglo-Saxons, having come from the continent, must have thought the connection natural. If the Synod had not happened in 664 it probably would have done so soon after and with the same outcome.

8

Cuthbert in Life and Death

Cuthbert's direct connection with Holy Island began when he was sent here, by Eata, Abbot of Melrose and Lindisfarne, to be prior. He was never abbot: the prior was the abbot's deputy and responsible to him.

Cuthbert on Lindisfarne

The Lindisfarne monks (who were now all English monks who had decided to accept the decision of the Synod of Whitby) were not happy to see him. They were probably happy enough to have Eata as their abbot, for he was one of their own, a Lindisfarne alumnus. But who was this unknown Cuthbert who now seemed to have a measure of authority over them? We are not given any of the details of the changes Cuthbert wished to introduce, but perhaps they included a stricter manner of life; perhaps some of the Island monks still wished to live by the usages they had known in the past (VP xvi). Cuthbert's method of dealing with this shows something of his character. He was determined never to quarrel with them. He held daily Chapter meetings in which he took the chair; he came in smiling and when the opposition grew too vitriolic he calmly walked out. The next day he did the same, just as if nothing had been wrong the previous day. He remained cheerful: Cuthbert's cheerfulness seems to have been one of his outstanding qualities. So gradually he either wore the opponents down or convinced them, and the monastery functioned as he wished.

He continued to be a man of prayer and asceticism. He had always been a person of physical strength and energy who enjoyed doing various jobs of the manual kind. But increasingly at this stage the story turns to his pastoral care. Some of this was in preaching, which he continued to do for people in nearby areas. But the emphasis comes now on to his gift of spiritual healing, which was seen as one of the charismatic gifts of the Holy Spirit, signs of sainthood. He could heal physical, mental and emotional illnesses and drive out demons. He was much sought as a confessor, capable of showing real empathy with those struggling with evil, even to the point of shedding more tears than the penitent. He was a man who did not mind showing emotion: when celebrating Mass he would often be overcome with tears, both of penitence and of longing for the life of union with God. But Bede also emphasizes his 'ordinariness': he wore ordinary clothes and was neither elegant nor slovenly. The physical details of his life, such as his sleeping arrangements, were exactly the same as those of the rest of the monks.

This life went on for a number of years, perhaps about ten. (Getting an exact chronology is not possible.) He must have become very well known on the near mainland, and very popular. To a man of his strongly compassionate nature it must have been a fulfilling way of life. Then, we suppose when he was about 40, everything changed because he began to think that God was calling him to be a hermit, to go and live alone.

Cuthbert as hermit (VP xvii–xxiv)

The hermit vocation was generally accepted at the time to be the hardest of all Christian vocations, but yet to be the most important. The essential task of the hermit was to be one of God's frontline soldiers in the most difficult war of all, the heavenly warfare against the forces of spiritual evil. The hermit was called to allow this warfare to be waged in and around him, as he trusted in God for strength but had no human help. By prayer and fasting alone he must fight this battle, for these were the only true Christian weapons. But if he won, that is, if he remained faithful, the spiritual benefit for the whole Church would be enormous. So it was no selfish vocation. The hermit was not cultivating his own soul. Cuthbert, and his fellow-Christians at the time, would genuinely have believed that if God was really calling him he must go, and that if he went in obedience he would be doing more for other people than if he stayed on Lindisfarne and healed a few hundred.

It must have caused some inner conflict. He cared so much for other people and had so much to give them. Yet there was the pull of the love of God, of the desire for growth in God's presence in the stillness and the aloneness, and the desire above all to do God's will. So Cuthbert chose as his first attempt at the hermit life the tiny island just a few yards from the south-west tip of Holy Island, which is called either Hobthrush or St Cuthbert's Island to this day. This tiny island is cut off from Holy Island by the tide twice each day exactly as Holy Island is cut off from the mainland (but be warned: not at exactly the same times!). But it was not the right place for a hermitage. Cuthbert could see and hear the monks as they went about their daily tasks and he could have walked back at low tide, or the monks or other visitors could have walked to him. He needed somewhere more remote and he chose the island now called the Inner Farne. Of the group called the Farne Islands, which are mostly bare rock, the Inner Farne is the nearest to the mainland. There were probably three reasons for this choice. First, the monks were accustomed to this island and St Aidan and others had used it for short-term retreats; yet its position further out in the ocean opened it more than Lindisfarne to the wildness of the sea and the wind conducive to the prayer of a fighter. Second, unlike the other islands the Inner Farne does have a certain amount of soil, so it was possible to grow crops there. Up to a point Cuthbert could feed himself. Third, in his day the Inner Farne for some reason had a terrible reputation: it was reputed to be more thickly populated with demons than any other place in the area. But if a person's vocation is to fight the demons he will go where the demons are.

So Cuthbert went to the Inner Farne. A group of Lindisfarne monks went with him and helped him build his hermitage. It had to be in stone, of course: the island did not grow timber. He built a chapel and a dwelling-hut and surrounded both by a high wall. So when he was in the hermitage he could not be seen from outside nor could he spend his time looking at the view! The Lindisfarne monks withdrew and left him alone.

Cuthbert was a hermit for about the next ten years; it is not possible to be exact. So far as we know no one else lived on the island during that time, but he did have visitors. The monks of Lindisfarne visited and kept an eye on him. The ordinary people still wanted his pastoral gifts. So when the sea was calm enough (it often isn't) they went out to him in their little boats and found him still the same friendly and attentive person he had always been. He constructed a landing-place and beside it a guesthouse for anyone who needed to rest there. Of course both monks and people would bring gifts of food. Increasingly though, as the years wore on, Cuthbert remained in his enclosure and spoke to his guests only through a window.

Then, when he was about 50 years old, a vacancy arose for a bishop following Archbishop Theodore of Tarsus' subdivision of the huge northern diocese. Everyone wanted Cuthbert. Without his consent or even knowledge he was elected bishop and allotted the see of Hexham. King Ecgfrith (Oswiu's son who had succeeded him) and the church authorities went out to the Inner Farne, told him what had happened and begged him to accept. At first he refused and seems to have agreed only when Eata, then Bishop of Lindisfarne, offered to take Hexham instead.

Cuthbert as bishop (VP xxiv–xxvi; xxix–xxxvii)

So Cuthbert became the sixth Bishop of Lindisfarne. He left the hermitage and for just under two years became a travelling and evangelizing bishop like Aidan, except that he did ride a horse when he thought it necessary. During this time we hear of him in many places. In fact Bede shows Cuthbert's life as bishop to have been one of constant activity, continual journeying. Much of this was in the area now called the Scottish lowlands, and we are told that he penetrated into country where no Christian missionary had gone previously. Usually he travelled in the company of at least one priest, visiting the villages, preaching, confirming those recently baptized and performing many miracles of healing.

Today the readers of these stories will be divided between those for whom the gift of spiritual healing is a reality, from their own experience and that of those they know, and those for whom this kind of narrative creates a lot of questions. Obviously we no longer have the evidence to discuss the 'truth' of these stories about Cuthbert. The sheer bulk of the story-material of healings, much greater than that claimed for any other of our saints, needs to be accounted for. Often the story will resemble Jesus' miracles in the Gospels. But that is to be expected, since the whole point of the saint was his closeness to his Lord. That closeness, in order that Jesus can work through his saint, is the particular concern of the narrator, in this case Bede.

For example, one of these stories very strongly resembles that of Peter's mother-in-law (Mark 1.29–31). A nobleman's wife, so ill that she was unconscious and unaware of the miracle that was being performed, was healed when Cuthbert blessed water which a priest then sprinkled over her, and poured a little into her mouth. She got up straightaway and served them. Another is reminiscent of a story in Luke's Gospel (Luke 7.11–16): once, in a mountainous district, when they were all in tents because there was no building, Cuthbert preached to the crowd and confirmed; women appeared carrying a dying youth on a pallet. Cuthbert gave his blessing and the youth was cured.

Other stories are related to actual conditions of Cuthbert's time: during an outbreak of bubonic plague (endemic at this period) Cuthbert, having helped all he could, looked to see if there was anyone else; there was a woman, whose older child had already died, holding a dying baby. Cuthbert cured the baby, kissed it and assured the mother that no one else in her household would die. At another time he visited a small group of nuns in a village house which he had previously given to them when they fled from a barbarian army. One of them had a severe pain in the head and one side. Cuthbert anointed her with holy oil and in a few days she recovered completely. One healing is interesting because it took place at a distance: a reeve (an official) was at the point of death when one of his friends remembered that he had some bread which Cuthbert previously had blessed. The group were all laymen, but devout and convinced that the bread could work a miracle. So they put a little in water; the dying man drank it and recovered.

Another story, not a miracle of healing, was told to express the saint's likeness to the Lord. He was with a community of nuns (a double house) 'at the mouth of the Tyne' where the Abbess Verca was a particular friend of his. At his request they gave him water to drink and then two others, men of this community, drank from the same cup. To them it tasted like wine, the best wine ever, and one of those two told the story to Bede.

Cuthbert at Carlisle

Bede knows of two visits of Cuthbert to Carlisle during his time as bishop. On the first of these, when he was being shown round the Roman ruins (VP xxvii) he had a sudden 'attack' of 'second sight'. King Ecgfrith, more bellicose than his father Oswiu, had led an expedition north of the Firth of Forth, which itself at that time was the northern boundary of Northumbria, to attack the Picts. The wily Picts lured him on up the mountains to a place called Nectansmere and there they turned on the English army and massacred them. At that moment Cuthbert in Carlisle 'knew' that Ecgfrith and most of his army were dead. As it happened Ecgfrith's queen was also in Carlisle, waiting in her sister's monastery for news of the Pictish expedition. So it fell to Cuthbert to inform her of this tragedy. Later she became a nun herself in the same religious house.

Cuthbert's second visit to Carlisle was to attend this queen's clothing as a nun and also to ordain priests. He managed to fit in one encounter which was more personal. For some years he had been friendly with a hermit, Hereberht, who lived on a small island in Derwentwater. They used to meet once a year for spiritual conversation, presumably usually at Lindisfarne or on the Inner Farne. Hearing that Cuthbert was in Carlisle Hereberht came to meet him there. But the conversation contained some bad news for the hermit: Cuthbert had forewarning of his own death and knew that this was their last meeting. Hereberht was devastated and begged not to outlive Cuthbert but to die on the same day. Cuthbert prayed for this and received heavenly reassurance: they would take their last journey on the same day. Hereberht had a much longer illness than Cuthbert, says Bede, because he needed more spiritual purification, but both in fact died on 20 March 687 at the same time (VP xxviii).

St Herbert's Isle can still be seen in Derwentwater.

The death of Cuthbert

In the anonymous *Life* the account of Cuthbert's last days is very brief. But Bede had the advantage of the testimony of Herefrith, Abbot of Lindisfarne, who was present on the Inner Farne when Cuthbert died and told him the story in detail (VP xxxvii–xxxix).

Cuthbert had a strong presentiment of his coming death. After he had spent what proved to be his last Christmas with the brothers at Lindisfarne he got out his little boat to go to his hermitage. Asked by one of the monks when they would see him again he replied sombrely, 'When you bring my body back here for burial.' Nonetheless he had two months of peace in which to re-establish the previous routine of his hermit life. It is very clear that the Lindisfarne monks visited frequently, staying in the guesthouse near the landing-place but not going into Cuthbert's enclosure. As it happened, Herefrith with some other monks was there when his final illness began for, when

Herefrith went to Cuthbert's window to ask for his blessing, it appeared that the saint had been taken ill during the night, not with the old trouble he had suffered ever since he got the plague at Melrose but with some new form of illness. Cuthbert persuaded Herefrith and the others to go home to Lindisfarne as arranged, but began to give instructions for his own burial. He wished to be buried on the Inner Farne, wrapped in a cloth his friend the Abbess Verca had given him and placed in a stone sarcophagus provided by another friend, the Abbot Cudda. So Herefrith went back to Lindisfarne, no doubt very worried.

Then for five days there was a tempest and no one could reach the Inner Farne. When Herefrith managed to get back there he found Cuthbert in the guesthouse by the landing place, where he had remained immobile for those five days, enduring bodily pain and the worst attacks of his spiritual enemies. He had five onions with him but had eaten only half of one onion during those days. Herefrith consulted the brothers who were with him and then asked Cuthbert's permission to take his body back to Lindisfarne. Cuthbert explained two objections: he would like to be buried on the little island where he had battled for the Lord and he would like to spare the Lindisfarne Community troubles, such as law breakers of all kinds seeking sanctuary at his body and needing to be helped. But finally he agreed, suggesting that his body should be within the church at Lindisfarne, so that the monks could at least lock the door!

Cuthbert then asked to be carried back to his oratory and allowed just one monk, a sick man who was immediately cured, to go in with him. Finally Herefrith and others were allowed in. Cuthbert's last words were an encouragement to the monks to keep the peace among themselves and preserve the unity of Catholic teaching. At the time of night prayer he received absolution, anointing and Holy Communion, and died in the act of praising God.

Then a brother went up to the highest point of the Inner Farne and waved two torches through the night in the direction of Lindisfarne. This was a pre-arranged signal and a brother in the lookout at Lindisfarne (on the Heugh or on Beblowe Hill?) picked up the signal and went to the monastery to tell the rest that Cuthbert was dead. The next day a boat brought Cuthbert's body back to Lindisfarne. Bede says that it was received by a great company and by choirs of singers, and was placed in a stone sarcophagus in the church of the blessed Apostle Peter on the right side of the altar.

The finding of the body

Even before he died Cuthbert had been looked on by many as a saint. Apart from his personal goodness and life of prayer and asceticism he exhibited so many of the 'gifts of the Spirit'. He had converse with angels, the gift of spiritual healing, the gifts of prophecy and second sight, the ability to read thoughts; then there was his life as a holy hermit, his time as a bishop. It was natural for some people to try to keep contact with him after his death by coming over to Lindisfarne to pray at his tomb.

Some of them received miracles there. Our records relate the story of a boy who was violently possessed, howling, groaning and gnashing his teeth, impervious to the rite of exorcism, then brought by his father to Lindisfarne and, on the inspiration of one of the priests, given some water in which a small piece of earth had been placed. That earth had been taken from the place where the water in which Cuthbert's dead body had been washed was poured away. The boy immediately became calm and quiet and was completely healed (VP xli).

If a person on earth can do such miracles he has the gift of healing, but if he can do them after death he is a saint in heaven. The Lindisfarne Community proceeded to an action which has been understood by many historians as the equivalent of 'canonization', the declaration of a person's sainthood. At that time saints were not made by a process at Rome. It was up to the local community to declare that they had a saint. This local process was 'elevation', the raising of the saint's physical relics and their re-interment at a place where pilgrims could see them, perhaps touch them, and pray very near them, for the theory was that the saint in heaven would give the supplicant a miracle via his/her earthly remains.

If this was indeed the intention of the Lindisfarne Community it is likely that they made long preparation for the elevation of Cuthbert's remains. They left the body to decay naturally until only a skeleton would remain. They calculated that 11 years would be the right time. He had died on 20 March 687, so 20 March 698 was the date fixed. It would be a great celebration, for 'elevation' was the joyful declaration of a saint.

The strange feature of the situation, which may count against the theory of 'elevation', was that the bishop did not plan to be present. He was not far away. March 20th is always in Lent and Bishop Eadberht gave permission for the dis-interment to go ahead, but he was in Lenten retreat, though only on the little island now called 'St Cuthbert's', and he did not propose to break his Lenten retreat. It seems almost inconceivable that the bishop should not be present if a canonization was intended. So some historians have thought that perhaps the day was not expected to be so significant. Perhaps all that was intended was the moving of the body to another site.

No one, apparently, was expecting what actually happened. When the coffin was brought up and opened there was no skeleton: instead there was a whole body, looking like a man asleep, exactly as he had looked when they buried him, his limbs flexible and his clothing uncontaminated by decay. They rushed to tell the bishop what they had found. The body was placed in a light chest, already prepared for the bones, and laid on the floor of the sanctuary. The miracles continued. A very sick man who had come over from Frisia was healed by praying beside the body; a paralysed man was healed by wearing the shoes in which the saint had been buried. It happened that Bishop Eadberht himself died soon after, so he was buried in the grave which St Cuthbert's body had vacated and the chest containing the saint's relics was laid on top (VP xlii–xlv).

For the monastic community this was the point in their story in which all changed. They could understand their discovery in only one way: that God had worked a great miracle to show the greatness of St Cuthbert as a saint. Whatever they had called themselves before, they now became 'St Cuthbert's Community'. The discovery of the body gave the monks the best possible relic any community could have. We must never underestimate the power of that body to them. It was not seen as a piece of dead human flesh. Rather, it was the means by which the saint still lived with his own people at the same time as he lived in heaven. He could still be approached by them and could still exercise his healing power. Through his body he could still, personally, receive their gifts, whether precious objects or lands. Much of the subsequent story is the story of the close connection between the saint, his body, his community and his lands. These four things go together. Wherever they travelled the body travelled with them. Without the body it is less likely that the community could have held together as they did through many later trials; without the body it is less likely that they could have maintained possession of their lands, or an entitlement to that possession. I should say, of course, St Cuthbert's lands, to emphasize that they were given to the saint himself, and I do mean after his death.

Hermits after Cuthbert

After the death of Cuthbert his hermitage on the Inner Farne was occupied in succession by two monks.

The first of these was Aethelwald. Earlier for many years he had been a monk and priest at Ripon, but when he wished to move to St Cuthbert's oratory on the Inner Farne the Lindisfarne Community adopted him as their own. He found the oratory in a ruinous condition: cracks and holes in the walls allowed the stormy winds to blow right through. St Cuthbert had been too heavenly minded to do more than take straw or clay or anything he could find to stuff up the cracks. But Aethelwald asked the brothers who visited him to bring a calf-skin, which he fixed in the corner where he usually prayed. Anyone who has experienced our winds will sympathize.

This hermit is credited also with a miracle of stilling a storm. The story was told to Bede by Guthfrith, first a pupil and later Abbot at Lindisfarne, who was one of the monks involved. He and two other brothers had visited Aethelwald in his hermitage on a calm day, but as they left a ferocious storm blew up and they could row neither forward nor back to the hermitage. But they could see Aethelwald who had come out of his hermitage to see what was happening to them. He knelt and prayed, and as his prayer ended the tempest calmed just sufficiently for the monks to reach home; after that it raged furiously all day.

Aethelwald was a hermit on the Inner Farne for 12 years and died there. His body was brought over to Lindisfarne and buried in the church of St Peter.

Bede tells also of the next hermit there, Felgild. At this point the bishop was Eadfrith, the artist of the Lindisfarne Gospels. He intervened and decided to restore the oratory completely, perhaps as part of his programme of promoting the cult of St Cuthbert. Enter the relic-hunters, asking for some relic of either Cuthbert or Aethelwald. Since Felgild, in his now windproof (!) oratory, had no use for the calf-skin, he decided to divide it among them, but first he tried an experiment. He suffered, it seems, from some rash or swelling of the face, which had got worse since he had taken up the solitary life. So he put part of this calf-skin into water and washed his face with it. All the disfigurement disappeared. Bede had this story from a devout priest in his own monastery who had seen Felgild's face before and after!

Felgild afterwards lived as a hermit there for many years, in complete freedom from this affliction, but nothing more is known of him (VP lxvi).

There may have been many more hermits at this time than we know. For example, in the colophon to the Lindisfarne Gospels added to the main text by the priest Aldred in the tenth century we are told that a hermit, Billfrith, put the jewels on the beautiful book's leather covers. We have no idea whether this Billfrith was a hermit on Lindisfarne or elsewhere, or how he came to have this skill. (The jewelled cover disappeared at the time of the Reformation, or it might have told us more about Billfrith.) With his name is coupled that of another hermit, Baldred, whose hermitage was on the Bass Rock in the Firth of Forth. He is credited with having prayed successfully for the removal of a dangerous reef from between the Bass Rock and the mainland to its present less perilous position. It is still known as Baldred's Rock. I understand that there is a tradition in that area that Baldred had a connection with Lindisfarne. There may have been many others who kept alive the ideals of austerity, devoted prayer and spiritual warfare against evil.

9

From Lindisfarne to Durham

The beginning of the cult of St Cuthbert

In the same year that St Cuthbert's body was discovered to be undecayed (in 698), Eadfrith became Bishop of Lindisfarne and held that office until his death in 721. It fell to him to promote the cult of St Cuthbert. Perhaps this cult had begun even before the discovery of the uncorrupt body. He seems to have been regarded as a saint even before his death. But the discovery of the body decided the matter: God had worked this miracle to show that he was a saint. It then became a duty as well as a joy for his community to promote this, to tell the world about Cuthbert. 'Canonization' was left to the local community.

So the Lindisfarne monks would have proclaimed their saint even if there had been no rival. But there was, for there was St Wilfrid. He had been a powerful person in his lifetime (died 709), though unpopular with other powerful people, especially kings. He had founded a monastic empire and had many followers. Although Wilfrid had been personally austere he had believed that the church should be as impressive as possible. He had built magnificent buildings for his time and travelled with a certain amount of pomp. After he died, almost immediately his very devoted follower, Eddius Stephanus, wrote his *Life*. How seriously we should take the idea of rivalry between his followers and Lindisfarne is not clear. But if the Community of St Cuthbert wanted to promote their saint they had to act, and act they did.

Lindisfarne was friendly with the monastery of Wearmouth/ Jarrow even though their lifestyles were different. Eadfrith was personally friendly with Bede. Previously, in about the year 704 or 705, Eadfrith had encouraged an anonymous monk of Lindisfarne to write a *Life of Cuthbert*, but now he wanted Bede to write the definitive hagiography. Bede was already regarded as the top scholar of the area; he had earlier shown an interest in St Cuthbert by writing an account of him in rather difficult Latin verse; he accepted Eadfrith's invitation, came to Lindisfarne to gather his material, no doubt talked to all the people he could, and wrote the *Life*, drawing on the existing anonymous work and adding further material to it; he wrote in a more elegant Latin style. Bede had a genuine devotion to St Cuthbert and, ten years after Eadfrith's death, he incorporated more about the saint into his last work, the *Ecclesiastical History*.

One of the precious objects the Wilfrid Community possessed was a lovely Gospel book, written in gold letters on purple parchment. Eadfrith, who was immensely gifted artistically, set out to give the Lindisfarne Community a very special book: the Lindisfarne Gospels. The whole book, writing and painting, except for minor details, is the work of Eadfrith. It was made 'for God and St Cuthbert'. For details of the art the reader is referred to one of the several books which reproduce the paintings. Here we can simply say that it is now thought of as a major treasure of the early Anglo-Saxon period. (Wilfrid's book has not survived.)

This superb book was not made for everyday use. It reposed on the altar near the shrine, for use only on special occasions. But for ordinary pilgrims, who could not read, its mere existence was laden with mystique: here was a book which somehow contained the Gospel of the Lord Jesus Christ. Even for those who could read and write Latin easily the written text had the power of the gospel in it. Words, spoken or written, were power-laden things.

The Gospels were not the only work of art to come from Lindisfarne at this time. The wooden coffin in which St Cuthbert's body was placed was covered with carvings of angels and saints; the pectoral cross which was hung round his neck is a beautiful piece of jewellery. We are in the period which has been called 'The Golden Age of Northumbria' because in matters of culture it led the rest of England. When we look at the objects which have survived we can only imagine the beauties which have been lost. It is most unlikely that the Lindisfarne Gospels was the only lovely book to come from the scriptorium on Lindisfarne.

But the age was coming to an end and in part this was because of political change: the eighth century was not to be like the 'golden' seventh.

Political change

A very remarkable feature of Northumbria in the seventh century had been that it was ruled for over 100 years by members of one family. There is no parallel to this elsewhere in Anglo-Saxon England. Aethelfrith became king in 592; he was succeeded by his cousin (though enemy) Edwin; then Aethelfrith's sons Oswald and Oswiu; then Oswiu's sons Ecgfrith and Aldfrith, who died in 704. He was succeeded by his son Osred but the days of success were over. All these kings from Edwin onwards were Christians and from Oswald onwards all supported the mission based on Lindisfarne.

Aldfrith's influence may have been important in the growth of the 'Golden Age'. He was born of some kind of liaison, marriage or otherwise, between the young Oswiu and an Irish lady called Fina. She came from the uppermost family of the uppermost Irish clan, the sons of Niall. She was probably sister to Finan, the second Bishop of Lindisfarne who followed Aidan. Bede's opinion is that Aldfrith was illegitimate and that is why his younger brother Ecgfrith became king on their father's death. Certainly Oswiu, on becoming king, felt no barrier then to taking a wife, Edwin's daughter Eanflaed.

Aldfrith was academically very able and studious; he was good enough at Latin to understand the writings of his friend

97

Aldhelm, usually thought to be the most complicated writer of Latin among the Anglo-Saxons; he was good enough at Irish to make a name for himself in Ireland as a poet. It seems that as an adult he lived in Ireland, no doubt keeping out of the way of his fratricidal brother Ecgfrith. He was even thinking of becoming a monk on Iona when that brother and his army were annihilated by the Picts at Nectansmere in 685. Aldfrith was then called to the throne of Northumbria.

By this time, although we do not know his age, he may well have been an old man of forty-plus so was not expected to lead an army in person. Through his loyal nobles he did at least hold the boundaries: his kingdom did not increase during his reign but neither did it diminish. As on old man of forty-plus he married and had sons, though sadly he did not live to see them grow up. The astonishing thing is, at a time when most kings were illiterate, Northumbria had a real scholar on the throne. Many people know the story of how the later Frankish emperor Charlemagne struggled to become literate, and later still the boy Alfred did the same. Why have so few people even heard of Northumbria's learned king, Aldfrith?

During the eighth century the political situation changed considerably and of course this had consequences for the community on Lindisfarne. For the kingship the eighth was a time of turmoil, a story of murders, depositions, abdications, with no one able to found a dynasty and some pretenders not even of the blood royal. There were reasons for this instability. One, no doubt, was the lack of the same quality and personal stature of their predecessors, for the seventh century Northumbrian kings had all been very remarkable men. But another reason was lack of land with which a king could reward his faithful followers. Northumbria could maintain its frontiers but it could no longer expand. To the south Mercia was growing in power and would in time take over Northumbria's previous position as the dominant Anglo-Saxon kingdom. To the north the Picts had proved their strength. So fresh land was not available for the kings to reward their men. Land given to a noble might revert to the king when that noble died, but in Northumbria so much land had been given to the Church, which never died and could never be conquered. Among the lands given to the Church the biggest share was given to St Cuthbert. So the Lindisfarne Community was right at the centre of this political problem. But a king without land to give was weak indeed. It is interesting that Bede, devoted monk though he was, at the end of his life (735) worried about the amount of land being given to the Church, partly because he believed that fraudulent monasteries were being set up and partly because he looked to the future and saw the consequences for the fighting men, who would drift off elsewhere to a leader who could reward them and so leave the land defenceless.

In the course of the eighth century there are glimpses, but no more than glimpses, of Lindisfarne and its Community. Among all the turmoil and the political wrangling the monastery would sometimes have had to take sides. For example, in 729 Ceolwulf became king; Bede clearly thought he was a good man, but was full of foreboding about his reign. After just two years as King Ceolwulf was seized and forcibly tonsured: a hint from his enemies perhaps? He managed to regain and rule his kingdom until 737. Then he voluntarily, but probably reluctantly, abdicated and became a monk at Lindisfarne, where eventually he gained a reputation for sanctity. But the presence of a controversial figure could hardly have promoted the peace of the monastery. The next king, Eadbert, Ceolwulf's cousin, was much more active and warlike. He was determined to exterminate the family of Aldfrith, whose son Offa had taken refuge at St Cuthbert's shrine in St Peter's church on Lindisfarne. Eadbert first imprisoned the bishop, Cynewulf, at Bamburgh because he would not hand Offa over. Then Eadbert besieged the church at Lindisfarne until Offa, starving and exhausted, was dragged from sanctuary. It is to be expected that monasteries would not be able to avoid this kind of involvement, since after all their men belonged to the same families as the contenders for the kingship. But it is interesting that this kind of trouble over Offa is exactly the sort of thing the dying Cuthbert foresaw when he wanted his body buried on the Inner Farne and no shrine to him on Lindisfarne.

But then these comparatively small incidents were swallowed up in the big incident at the end of the century.

The Viking attack

We shall probably not know in detail what happened on that fateful day in 793, the Viking attack on Lindisfarne. *The Anglo-Saxon Chronicle* gives the date as 8 January. Some historians have thought this unlikely, as the Vikings did not usually go a-viking in the winter, and so they have suggested 8 June. An alternative suggestion is that they had actually crossed the seas earlier and had been hiding out, ready for their planned attack. Was it in fact a planned attack? A suggestion has been made that they were heading somewhere else and were blown off course. But the Vikings probably did have good intelligence; they were pagans but they knew that in a monastery they would find unarmed men, silver and gold booty and, if they wanted them, slaves.

The attack on Lindisfarne was preceded, so the *Chronicle* says, by 'terrible portents over Northumbria . . . exceptional flashes of lightning . . . fiery dragons seen flying in the air' and then 'the heathen miserably destroyed God's church . . .' It seems clear that some monks were killed, probably some were taken to be sold as slaves and that some of the monastery was burned. But not everything: the body in its coffin survived, as did the Lindisfarne Gospels, so it has been speculated that the monks did have enough warning to hide their most precious treasures.

It was not the end of the Community of St Cuthbert. But the attack did cause shock waves in some parts of Christian Europe. Our best evidence for this is the correspondence of Alcuin, a Northumbrian scholar of York who had been enticed by the Frankish Emperor Charlemagne to his court, to become a leading light in the revival of learning there. Alcuin was shattered by the news. He wrote, 'The church of St Cuthbert is spattered with the blood of the priests of God . . . stripped . . . exposed . . . a place more sacred than any in Britain'. Whose fault was it? Obviously in one sense, St Cuthbert's. What would happen to the rest of the churches if so great a saint, accompanied by all the other Lindisfarne saints, did not defend his own centre? But there must have been a reason and Alcuin looks for it in the moral sphere. He advises the surviving monks to examine themselves and their way of life and repent and reform. The Community did survive, though no doubt never with the old confidence.

Leaving the Island

The Vikings were the best seafarers anyone had experienced and as their attacks continued, up and down the coast of England, Scotland, Ireland and the continent, it seemed good sense to move away from the sea. It is likely that the lands of Islandshire (the mainland nearest to the Island) and Norhamshire (round the lower reaches of the River Tweed) had been early gifts to the Lindisfarne monastery, perhaps in the seventh century. It was to Norham that the community now looked for greater safety. There is a tradition that during the time of Bishop Ecgred (830–845) a church was built there which housed the relics of King Ceolwulf and eventually, and briefly, housed the body of Cuthbert. But this body, if taken to Norham, seems to have been taken back to the Island before the final move away.

The final move was perhaps precipitated by a number of considerations. The Vikings hitherto had been raiders rather than settlers. But in 865 the so-called Great Army of the Danes invaded. Although, in the north, York and Yorkshire were to be the main area of settlement, in 874 the northern Danish leader, Halfdan, wintered on and around the mouth of the Tyne. So it was feared that North Northumbria would be occupied. But the monks may have been disturbed also by a movement of the Picts southwards. In any case, so much of their land was now to the south of Lindisfarne that it might have seemed good sense to live more centrally among their possessions. If they had been motivated by fear of the Vikings alone why did they move nearer to the centre of Viking power at York? But whatever were their reasons, in 875 the Lindisfarne monks decided to leave the Island. They took with them the body, the Lindisfarne Gospels, the head of King Oswald, some of the bones of St Aidan, some of the bones of Eadfrith, and other relics.

The community which left the Island in 875 was powerful, wealthy and streetwise. It was not a flight, it was a planned relocation. We must get rid of the romantic idea of a few tattered monks manhandling St Cuthbert's body round the country haphazardly. If that is what the sources suggest it is because the chronicler's intention is to play down the living human factor and emphasize the role of the saint himself in every decision. Bishop Eardwulf, assisted by his friend Eadred, Abbot of Carlisle, led them over to Carlisle. It seems that they considered moving to Ireland, where no doubt many a monastery would have been glad to receive them. But this plan was thwarted by St Cuthbert, who brought up a storm and turned water into blood. From there they went round the corner to Whithorn, then down to Crayke in Yorkshire, and finally up to Chester-le-Street. It has been pointed out that much of the land they crossed and visited belonged to them already, and so this progress round the country seems more like taking an opportunity to visit their outlying estates than a headlong flight from danger. Certainly in moving south they moved nearer to the Vikings. But St Cuthbert knew how to make friends with Vikings. The story is that he chose a certain Viking slave boy named Guthfrith, organized his release from slavery and then ordered his elevation to the kingship of Northumbria, in return for the gift of certain lands between the Tyne and the Tees. Cuthbert did all this through an appearance to the Abbot of Carlisle. There certainly was a Danish king at York, called Guthfrith, a Christian, who died in 895; so behind this story is probably a memory of an alliance between this king and St Cuthbert's Community, in which each side supported the other. If this king did give land as the story suggests, it makes sense of the choice of Chester-le-Street for their settlement, in the centre of this land.

At Chester-le-Street

It is possible that this old Roman town already had connections with the Community, perhaps as one of their staging-posts between Lindisfarne and York. They settled there in 883 and stayed for 112 years.

We are not sure, of course, that they intended to stay all that time. Throughout their stay their church was only a wooden one, yet they were in an old Roman town with plenty of Roman cut stones. Why did they not do as was done at Escomb, where a church was erected from the stones of a Roman fort? Perhaps they always intended to move on; perhaps they intended at some point to go back to the Island. They still possessed their lands in the north, though perhaps growing Scottish assertiveness would have made the north less comfortable. For whatever reason, they stayed. An important feature of these years is the friendship that grew up between the Kings of Wessex and St Cuthbert, who seems to have known which way England was developing. Cuthbert is said to have appeared to Alfred the Great, at his darkest moment as a refugee from the Danes, and foretold a great victory to come, no doubt promising help. Alfred at his death impressed upon his son, Edward the Elder, the need to revere St Cuthbert with suitable gifts and to assist the Community. Edward may have come to the shrine in person; his son Athelstan certainly did in 934, bringing costly gifts including land, books and jewels which he, in person, gave to St Cuthbert in person. It is likely that the later Wessex Kings Edmund and Eadred also came to the shrine. There is no need to doubt that these men were genuinely religious and genuinely believed in the presence and power of the saint. But they were also warriors and politicians and must have known that here, in St Cuthbert's Community, was one of the strongest political forces in the north, with which it would be good sense to ally.

During the years at Chester-le-Street the ex-Lindisfarne Community changed in a number of ways. One of these was a loss, or partial loss, of the traditional monastic values and way of life. It seems that the monks were replaced by secular clerics, for whom it was still quite legal to be married. By 995 they had a married bishop and they would have appeared more like a bishop's household than a monastery. This may have contributed to a loss of monastic culture generally, which shows itself in at least two ways. One is a worsening of the standards of stone-carving compared with earlier examples. The other is suggested by Aldred's Anglo-Saxon gloss on the Latin text of the Lindisfarne Gospels. Aldred was a priest of the Community and obviously a competent Latinist. He wrote, between the lines of the Lindisfarne Gospels, above each Latin word its equivalent in Anglo-Saxon. Did he do it because many in the Community were not as competent in Latin as the monks used to be? Or because English language, English culture, was growing in self-confidence and demanding to be used? Clearly Aldred considered that, far from spoiling the manuscript, he was doing a good work, and more recent scholars have been glad of it for this gloss is the oldest surviving translation of the Gospels into English, and is a gift to those who study the development of the language since it shows Northumbrian English shortly before the Norman Conquest. But Aldred probably had some immediate usefulness in mind. Perhaps he was considering that the group who escorted St Cuthbert's body through Northumbria included some lay people, who would not have known Latin. For the term 'people of the holy man' included all who lived on St Cuthbert's lands, of whom some may have been sufficiently devoted to wish to settle near his body. Such people are invisible in our records.

The final journey

The Danes who were resident in England appear to have subsided by the end of the tenth century. But there were still those who came a-viking from Scandinavia. It seems that renewed raids convinced Bishop Aldhun that Chester-le-Street was too near the coast. So he removed all his group of people, including the body, down to Ripon. But they did not stay long; possibly they judged that it had been a false alarm. So back they came north-eastwards from Ripon, which brings us to the most famous story of all, the choosing of the site of Durham. We can look at this in three ways. We can note, with most sober historians, that Bishop Aldhun was father-in-law to the local lord, Earl Uhtred; that the latter part of the journey back had been through land that belonged to this earl, as did the site of Durham; that this site was an excellent defensive position, an important matter while attack was still to be feared; and therefore it is obvious that the bishop and the earl decided it between them. Or, second, we can go along with the chronicler and say that St Cuthbert chose the spot, causing his body to become immovable and then disclosing to one of his followers that he wished to be buried at Dunholme (Durham's earlier name). And, third, we can add to this the two women, one of whom had lost her cow. We can allow the lost cow, which was repossessed on Dunholme, to indicate the site of the new shrine. We must be critical of our sources and rec-ognize that the cow is a late tradition, not in writing before the sixteenth-century book, *The Rites of Durham*. But every shrine needs a foundation legend and Durham has one of the best.

The cow had chosen well. Durham stood up to the turmoil of the next half-century. Attacks by Scots, chaos among the Northumbrian leaders, further Scandinavian invasions still left the Community of St Cuthbert with most of its influence and its extensive lands intact. In an age when many religious communi-ties had gone under, it had come through. To Norman eyes the group of married canons, lay people and who-knows-what-else which was now the Community appeared strange. But it was not the pathetic group of survivors of some people's imagination.

But yet, in 1083, with the Normans now in power, the Nor-man Bishop William of St Carileph replaced it with a pukka Benedictine regime. The members of the old Community were offered the chance to join this; the records say that only one did and alternative futures were found for the others. Of course Bishop William wanted his new monastery to have the inheritance, that is, the body and the extensive lands. So the Benedictines claimed to be the rightful heirs of the Lindisfarne tradition. To do this they had to put the pre-1083 guardians of the body and the shrine, that is the members of the old Community, in a bad light. They read Bede; they knew that the house on Lindisfarne had originally been monastic, but they knew nothing of Irish monasticism or indeed of any monastic way other than the highly organized Benedictine. So they assumed that the less organized, more diverse group that they found guarding the shrine had fallen away from an earlier ideal, which they assumed to have been a Benedictine one. So this shameful decline must now be put right. The Benedictines must resume their rightful inheritance. So from this time on the guardians of the body and possessors of the lands are Durham Benedictine monks, no longer the Lindisfarne Community far from home.

Additional note: the Green Shiel site

Possibly the most exciting discovery made on the island by the Leicester archaeologists (see Chapter 1) was near the north shore on a site called Green Shiel. The remains of buildings were found which when uncovered were provisionally identified as dwelling houses with a byre and a barn, to be dated to the early/mid ninth century. This was an important discovery as most ninth-century remains in other places are either ecclesiastical or military; very few domestic buildings have been identified.

It had been known since the later nineteenth century that there were ruins in that place. When a wagonway was being constructed to carry limestone to the kilns (Chapter 11), some stones from these ruins were 'robbed' to be used in this construction. At that time two ninth-century Northumbrian 'stycas' were found: these are coins of extremely small value. No further interest was shown at the time. The sand of the dunes has concealed a good deal, but the dunes are comparatively recent. In the ninth century the settlement would have been surrounded by good arable land.

Preliminary work was done in 1980. The first task was to find some way of dating the site: the unearthing of an Anglo-Saxon spearhead of the late ninth or early tenth century provided the key dating. The task of excavation began in 1985 and lasted some years.

The buildings were in stone, probably from the nearby beach. At this time most domestic architecture was still wooden; perhaps these people found it hard to get wood which they would had preferred but, ironically, it was the fact that they used stone which enabled their building to survive. The construction was called 'haphazard'. The stones were roughly rectangular; there was no sign of mortar or clay, so the cracks were probably filled with turf or straw. It is thought that the buildings had pitched roofs, supported by a single line of posts down the centre.

The finds from the excavation do not include any pottery at all. This is typical of Northumberland, which seems to have managed without pottery after Roman times. That suggests that the people would have used wooden vessels, which then disintegrated leaving no trace. A number of animal bones were found, of which the majority were from cattle, but there were also bones of deer, seals and even a whale, which perhaps had become stranded. There were plenty of bird bones and range of fish. Fortunately no human bones were found (so the Coroner was not involved!). Surprisingly, five complete cattle carcases were found: two were buried together inside a building, one was buried in the inmost compartment of the 'byre' and an adult and a calf were apparently simply 'dumped' on the surface. There were also plenty of remains of limpets and winkles, which may have been used for bait rather than for human consumption.

Altogether 19 coins were found. Only one of these was of value: a silver penny of Ethelred, King of Wessex 866–71. The rest were stycas, mostly scattered. Seven were found together: someone's precious collection, though not worth much. They show that coins were in use, though it is not clear what they were used for.

Other finds are quite meagre: a large iron key, but to lock what? A single amber bead was the only personal ornament. There were fragments of a bone comb, pieces of bronze for binding, two small iron knives.

At first it was thought that this could have been a farming settlement, with perhaps three families and space for animals, possibly completely unconnected with the monastery. If that were so it would be the only evidence for lay people living on the Island during the time of the first monastery. But completion of the excavation has suggested another possibility. The crude state of the buildings, the lack of reasonable provision for fire-places and the lack of evidence of domestic life indicate that this was not for family occupation. The large quantity of cattle remains might indicate a 'specialized construction site', possibly to breed young cattle for their skins and the making of parchment. Such activity could be seasonal, in which the workers could put up with rough conditions; and it would suggest that this site was part of the monastic economy, not independent of it.

It is thought that the site was not in use for long, and there is nothing which post-dates the departure of the monks in 875. So it gives no answer to the question, 'Did anyone live on the Island after the monks left?'

10

The Benedictine Years

The Benedictine tradition

The second monastery on Holy Island, now to be seen in ruins, was a daughter-house or 'cell' of the newly established Benedictine community in Durham. It brought to the Island a monastic tradition which differed in some major ways from the Irish tradition brought by St Aidan and the monks of Iona. St Benedict of Nursia, who lived in Italy from about 480 to about 547, belonged to the experimental period in early monasticism, when individual houses were free to develop in their own ways. In each house the abbot was the supreme authority; some abbots wrote Rules for their monks; others preferred to be living Rules themselves and to deal with situations as they arose. Benedict's most famous monastery was at Monte Cassino near Naples. Probably with just this one monastery in mind, and having no idea of founding an Order, he wrote his Rule in about the year 515. But this Rule was so humane, so balanced that, as it became known, so it became popular. It was adopted by many other Religious Houses, at first often alongside other Rules of their own, but was to become by the tenth century the dominant monastic Rule in western Europe. The Benedictine Order retained this dominance until it was challenged first by developments within its own tradition, such as the Cistercians, and then by various new forms of the Religious Life, such as the Orders of Friars.

This Benedictine way of life had many virtues. It demanded the sinking of individual preferences into the common life of the community, so that all the monks rose, ate, worshipped and worked together, at the same times. To Benedict this sacrifice of the individual will was the real discipline of the community. But in his preface to his Rule Benedict had said that he wanted 'a little school for beginners in which there should be nothing harsh or burdensome'. So the physical life of the monks was well cared for, with sufficient food, clothing and sleep. It was a well-balanced Rule with work, prayer and spiritual reading in each day's programme. It was an extremely well-thought-out system which deserved to succeed, and it is good to think that it has its place in the spiritual tradition of our Island.

The founding of the Priory

The Benedictines of Durham came to the Island probably in the 1120s, first to build a church. It is not known whether anyone was living on the Island when they came, though a village certainly grew up alongside the monastery later. It may be conjectured that they found here a little stone church, the core of the present parish church of St Mary the Virgin, and that there was something to indicate the site of the earlier shrine of St Cuthbert which had been in St Peter's church. The Island now belonged to Durham, along with all the other property the Community of St Cuthbert had possessed. Durham had retained the incorrupt body of St Cuthbert and in 1104 had built for it a new shrine behind the high altar in the new Norman Durham Cathedral.

It is not clear whether the authorities at Durham intended at the first, when they built the church here, to have a group of monks on the Island. It has been pointed out, for instance, that when they built the church they did not allow very easy access into what would be the monastery. But what is quite obvious is that they built the church as a miniature copy of the great cathedral being constructed at Durham. The remains of the pillars show the same kind of decoration as at Durham. There was a stone vaulted roof as at Durham. Everything was done to make the connection, for Durham saw itself as the true inheritor of the Lindisfarne tradition. (It could have had something of a bad conscience about the way the Community of St Cuthbert had been despoiled and have wanted to justify itself in the eyes of the world.) However, in the relative sizes of the two buildings, the great cathedral there and the new little church here, Durham pointed out that the power was now in Durham.

But Holy Island church was, for its size, rather grand and elaborate. (We can now speak of 'Holy Island' for it was the Benedictines of Durham, with our saints and martyrs in mind, who renamed it 'the Holy Island of Lindisfarne', still its official name.) The materials for the Priory church had to be good. The chronicler Reginald of Durham says that the sandstone of the Island was not good enough, and that the lovely deep red sandstone we can still see in the church was brought over at low tide from quarries at Scremerston/Cheswick just up the coast. He says that the people of the area gave their carts and labour free because of love for St Cuthbert.

So the Benedictines intended to honour the original grave of St Cuthbert and to connect the Island to Durham. How they might have staffed the church had they not built a monastery we do not know. The monastic buildings date from the 1150s but there could have been monks resident here before then, living in temporary accommodation of which there is now no trace.

Holy Island as a Durham cell

The mother house at Durham eventually had nine 'cells', of which Holy Island was one. All the cells were staffed with Durham monks, who all spent their novitiate at Durham, took their vows to the Lord Prior there and then were sent out at his command. (The chief monk at Durham, who would have been called 'the abbot' elsewhere, was the Prior; the whole monastery, though huge, was a Priory not an Abbey. The reason for this is that the Bishop of Durham, even though normally not a monk, had the title of abbot. Through the Middle Ages there was a long and uneasy love/hate relationship between the Bishops and the Priors. But the Prior of Durham was often called the 'Lord Prior' to distinguish him from the lesser priors of the cells.) So all the monks had their allegiance firmly fixed to Durham itself, to the Lord Prior, and not to any cell. The Lord Prior appointed the priors of the cells and all the monks moved around at his command, simply on receipt of a letter from him with the details of their next move.

Most of the cells were fairly unpopular with the Durham monks, though they all had to spend part of their time in one or other of them. The two cells that were more popular were Durham College, Oxford, founded in the 1280s, and Finchale Priory, just a few miles along the river from Durham, which served as a rest and recuperation home. But the cell on Holy Island was especially unpopular with the monks. It is easy to see why. It felt like the edge of the world. What company was there except seals and seagulls? Back home in Durham they had one of the most beautiful churches in the world, one of the finest libraries, one of the best choirs. There they were connected with all the important goings-on and could keep up with the news. The site here, which had been so perfect for St Aidan and the Irish monks, might for all we know have suited a few individuals among the Benedictines, quiet men of good will who were able to live here in loyalty to their vows. Clearly the extent to which the life in general here was truly lived, the degree of faithfulness to the Rule, would depend a good deal on the character of the prior. But even for priors the average time here was only four years and many of the monks stayed for one year only. Also, there was a great temptation for the Lord Priors, since they had complete power in the matter, to send difficult monks to remote stations. A good man would resist this temptation, but there is evidence of some fear, from time to time, that it was happening.

1 View from the Island to the mainland with the snow-capped
Cheviot Hills in the distance. Mesolithic people would have
seen this as a flat plain.
Photo: Rachel Crick

2 The statue of St Aidan in St Mary's churchyard on the Island.
The sculpture is by Kathleen Parbury, 1958.
Photo: Lilian Groves

3 An impression of a
youthful St Cuthbert
from a window in St
Mary's church, Holy
Island. Designed by
Leonard Evetts.
Photo: Lilian Groves

4 A bronze cast of a wooden sculpture of St Cuthbert by Fenwick
Lawson, now standing in Lindisfarne Priory.
Photo: Rachel Crick

5 St Cuthbert's Island, where he was first a hermit, seen from
Holy Island at high tide.
Photo: Rachel Crick

6 The Wheel Cross by Fenwick Lawson, showing the face of
St Cuthbert. Now in the Gospels Garden on Holy Island.
Photo: Lilian Groves

7 The sculpture by Fenwick Lawson called The Journey, depicting the monks carrying the body of St Cuthbert away from the Island. Now in St Mary's church, Holy Island.
Photo: Lilian Groves

8 A view of St Mary's church in relation to the ruined Benedictine priory.
Photo: Rachel Crick

9 The Rainbow Arch: the most striking feature of the ruined
Benedictine monastic church.
Photo: Lilian Groves

10 In the foreground the embankment on which the
wagonway brought limestone to the kilns.
Photo: Enid Riley

11 The later set of lime kilns, near the Castle.
Photo: Lilian Groves

12 All that now remains of the jetty from which ships took the powdered lime.
Photo: Lilian Groves

13 The Pilgrims' Way, a safe approach on foot when the tide is out. Holy Island village is in the foreground.
Photo: Rachel Crick

14 The modern causeway: the only approach to the Island for wheeled traffic.
Photo: Rachel Crick

15 An honourable end to a life of fishing! One of the herring boats, sawn in two, now used for storage.
Photo: Rachel Crick

16 The priory ruins from St Mary's churchyard with the Castle in the background.
Photo: Rachel Crick

A Bishop of Durham from Holy Island?

At this point we mention one medieval Bishop of Durham who might have a closer connection with Holy Island than the rest. He was Bishop from 1274–83 and his name was Robert de Insula: 'Robert from the Island'. Whether his Island was in fact Holy Island is not completely sure but it is generally so understood.

Robert was not one of the outstanding bishops of Durham. Before his election he was Prior of Finchale. It is nice but a little romantic to imagine him as a child in the village here, perhaps fascinated by the monks and hanging round the monastery until someone noticed him and offered him education and he went on from there. During his time as bishop there were complaints about Scottish 'Border reivers' raiding in the bishopric, and Robert did what he could to help the people by laying the matter before the King, but the full Border Wars had not yet broken out. Otherwise his time as bishop seems to have been peaceful.

One rather endearing episode, whether true or not, concerns his mother, of whom he was very fond. When he became Bishop he established her in a house in Durham, with servants and everything she needed. He then asked her if she was happy. 'No!' she replied. 'Why not?' 'Because everyone here is so respectful to me, no one will contradict me, there is no one with whom I can argue!' So it could be that his mother was one of those strong-minded, independent Holy Island women, of whom everyone here has known a few.

Life in the Priory

The little monastery here was built on a normal Benedictine pattern. There was a village of lay people many of whom, as the years went by, were employed by the monastery. The monks did not expect these lay people to use the Priory church for their usual worship, so the little stone church, now St Mary's, was enlarged and became the parish church, as it is to this day. The Priory appointed and paid a chaplain to serve the parishioners.

But those lay people who came as pilgrims were allowed into the nave of the Priory church, as far as the rood screen at the foot of which there would have been a nave altar for the pilgrims' Mass. They would have entered the church by a special door on the north side, not by the west door, which was used only by monks and even by them only occasionally when they had processions. This pilgrims' door on the north side was blocked up about a century before the monastery was dissolved, indicating that pilgrimages had come to an end; though probably the Island was never a great centre for pilgrimage during these centuries. Pilgrims seem to have preferred to go either to Durham itself, where they could (if they were male) visit the shrine of St Cuthbert's body behind the high altar, or to go to the Inner Farne where St Cuthbert was for a number of years a hermit.

At Holy Island Priory the monks were expected to maintain the Benedictine round of prayer (seven services every 24 hours plus the Mass) and to live according to their Rule. Their important outer work was to manage the lands belonging to the mother house on the Island and the near mainland. (Durham's lands were so extensive that the management of them was normally the job of a strategically placed cell.) Some of these lands were allocated to the Holy Island monks for themselves, to live on the income and the tithes from these. It seems that this grant from Durham even at the beginning was somewhat mean, but each cell was expected to be self-sufficient. The prior of each cell had to keep accounts and travel to Durham once a year to submit accounts and inventories of their property to the authorities.

We are not sure how many monks were originally established here. The size of the buildings suggests perhaps a prior and 12 monks, but even at the start there may not have been quite so many, and as the years went by the numbers were reduced dramatically. Perhaps at first the life of the Priory was peaceful, although the Prior might always have had to cope with unwilling or even unruly members. But later there were major problems. Of these the worst and longest-lasting were the Border Wars with the Scots, which began in the 1290s. The monastery was too near to the border for comfort. Although the Scots were Christians they had a special reason to dislike this priory: the King of England's top military officers insisted on using it as their headquarters when they were in the area. So it would have been to Scottish advantage to destroy it. Knowing this the Prior and monks lived in fear, and took measures to protect themselves. Attack might come from the west, from the mainland, so the Prior for part of the time kept a lookout man on Snook point, the nearest bit of the Island to the mainland. The west wall of the church and its side towers, which contained staircases, were projected upwards; crossbow loops were placed for archers above the original line of the church roof, to 'pick off' any Scottish raiders coming from the west. Of course monks, as men of peace, were not expected to bear arms themselves and fight, but some of the men from the village were no doubt skilled archers. The great outer courtyard was constructed and crenellated and the door into the monastery itself from this courtyard became a fortified inner gateway. The plan appears to have been that, should a Scottish raiding party land on the Island, the villagers and their animals would come into the outer courtyard. Should the Scots capture this courtyard the animals would be abandoned and the village people would all come into the monastery itself through the fortified inner gateway. Then, presumably, they would try to hold out in the hope of being relieved by an English army. On the east side of the monastery attack might come from the sea, which was much closer to the monastery wall than it is now, as the harbour was much bigger. So the space on the east side of the 'warming house' was adapted to accommodate villagers, the east wall was reinforced and towers were provided for archers to stand invisibly and shoot through slits in the wall.

As far as we know there was no Scottish attack, apart from a certain William de Prendergast who in 1327 is said to have knocked down the kitchen wall. Perhaps the Scots were deterred by all these fortifications; perhaps they had a rational fear of the tides; perhaps they had a superstitious fear of St Cuthbert who during the High Middle Ages had changed in people's perception from being the compassionate man he actually was into being a ferocious defender of his property and his community. Perhaps it was simply enough for the Scots to destroy the crops every harvest-time on the monastic lands on the mainland, so substantially reducing the monastery's income. But all this preparation for an attack that did not happen had taken too much of the resources of the Priory. Perhaps the Black Death also had an effect: not, as far as we know, on the monks themselves but on the workers who were essential for supplying the income. (The Black Death was a particularly virulent outbreak of the bubonic plague in the mid fourteenth century, which in some places killed as many as half the people and had a devastating effect on the economic and social life of the nation.) So, inevitably, the number of monks went down, to eight, to six, and then in the last century before the Dissolution to just two or three. The monks at this point sensibly abandoned their now over-spacious dwelling quarters and adapted part of the south side of the building to live in.

King Henry VIII closed the small monasteries first, alleging that they were inefficient. He may well have been right by that time about Holy Island Priory. In 1537 the few remaining monks here were sent back to Durham and were probably glad to go. No one at that stage told them that Durham would be closed just two years later.

So ended 900 years of the story of Holy Island, for most of which monasticism was dominant. Although we know that there were those throughout England who did not lament its passing we can only guess that for ordinary people here, who for centuries had lived in the shadow of the monastery, the loss must have been mind-blowing. They did not know, of course, that this was to be a permanent loss. No one knew, in the reign of Henry VIII, that a major and enduring change in the religious life of the country had in fact occurred.

The hermits of the Inner Farne

Before we leave the Benedictine period we should glance across the sea to the Inner Farne, to the hermits who had been living there. The Christian monastic tradition had included hermits from the start; indeed the word 'monk' itself comes from the Greek word for 'alone' and the heroic first monks, whom we call the Desert Fathers, were many of them passionate solitaries. But as the tradition developed, both experience and wisdom suggested that it was best if those who became hermits were first fully experienced in the community life of the monastery, so as to establish their spiritual values and routines with the sensible help of others. This is still true today, where the hermits attached to the Religious Orders were first and for some years full community members in that Order.

Earlier (see Chapter 8) we mentioned Aethelwald and Felgild, hermits on the Inner Farne in the time of the first monastery on Lindisfarne. After them we do not know of other hermits until the Benedictine years. In 1255 the mother house at Durham established a cell on the Inner Farne (one of its nine daughter houses) with normally two members, both hermits, known as the Master and the Companion. But before 1255 there are two picturesque characters worth meeting, who have some connection with our story.

First, St Godric of Finchale. This remarkable man was born in Norfolk in 1069 and lived to the age of 101. At first he was a wanderer, alternating pilgrimages to Rome and Jerusalem with the life of a ship's captain, who may well have been also a pirate. He is even said to have taken his mother with him on some of his piratical expeditions. But one day one of his sea journeys took him to the Inner Farne and probably also to Lindisfarne, and he learned and was inspired by the story of St Cuthbert. He decided to be a hermit but for a while continued as a wanderer, trying various places. He eventually settled at Finchale, a little way along the River Wear from the Durham monastery. Here he lived a very austere life in a wooden hut, eating roots, berries and the few vegetables he grew. Once he was nearly drowned when the River Wear was in flood, and once he was nearly killed by a raiding party of Scots. But he survived and became renowned for his holiness and his psychic gifts. He cared a great deal for animals and in bad wintry weather would bring rabbits and field mice into his hut to warm them and then set them free. He was also a poet and a musician and set his own poetry to music.

He never exactly joined the Durham Community but the monks gave him friendly protection, nursed him in his last illness, took him to their heart and accepted him as their own. After his death a priory was built at his hermitage at Finchale, which eventually became a daughter house of Durham.

The second picturesque character is St Bartholomew of Farne. He was born in the early twelfth century near Whitby, of Scandinavian parents who called him Tostig, a name he soon discarded when the other boys laughed at him; he then called himself William. After a wild youth he had a vision of Christ and the apostles, went to Norway and was there ordained deacon and priest. Many priests in Norway were married; William fled back to England to avoid a marriage which was being forced on him. He became a monk at Durham and took the name Bartholomew. A further vision of St Cuthbert caused him to become a hermit on the Inner Farne. He lived there for the remaining 42 years of his life.

Although Durham had not yet formally set up 'the House of Farne', Bartholomew found a hermit already there: a certain Aelwin, who disliked his new companion and left. He was alone from about 1151–63, when he was joined by Thomas, Prior of Durham, deposed after a row with the Bishop. After a shaky beginning together the two became friends and Bartholomew nursed Thomas through his last illness.

Bartholomew was very austere, wearing skins, sleeping up against the rocks, living on bread from his own corn, milk from his own cow, and fish; he used to stride around the island singing psalms all the way in a ringing voice. He was also cheerful and friendly and had many visitors, including some of the rich and powerful whom he persuaded to change their oppressive ways. In his old age the monks of Holy Island cared for him as much as possible. He died in 1193 and was buried in his oratory on the Inner Farne. Miracles at his tomb showed he had reached the heavenly Kingdom.

When Durham had established the House of Farne cell in 1255 it maintained two hermits there until the Dissolution of the Monasteries under Henry VIII. The names of the Masters are extant and we have the name of one of the Companions. This was a hermit who wrote a series of meditations which have survived, been translated from Latin and published under the title *The Monk of Farne*. Writing meditations was considered to be an appropriate type of work for a hermit and no doubt many hermits composed them. This book has survived among the medieval manuscripts of Durham; it is the only surviving book, as far as we know, which was actually written on the Farne Island. We think we know the author's name: John Whiterig.

Of the details of his life we know little. He died at Farne in 1371, probably still under 50 years old. He entered the Durham Community in about 1350. Either before this, or soon after he entered, he studied at Oxford. Durham Priory encouraged the monks to do this and maintained a house at Oxford: Durham College, on the site of the present Trinity College. We know that John Whiterig was there as he tells of an incident when he very nearly fell off a bridge over the river Cherwell, to his probable death in the river below, but was saved (he believed) by his guardian angel. He visited the Farnes twice and Lindisfarne once before he settled as a hermit (the accounts including his expenses for these expeditions have survived). For some years at Durham he was novice master, then in 1363 he settled on the Inner Farne. A new house built there that year may have been for him.

His life coincided with a number of serious conflicts in the wider world. In 1346 the battle of Neville's Cross, just outside Durham, resulted in a victory for the English against the Scots, but the Border Wars were by no means over. In the wider church

the strange period where there were two Popes, one at Rome
and one at Avignon, with Christians taking sides, was not con-
cluded until 1378. At Oxford John would have met a good deal
of controversy about grace and pre-destination, and he may
have known Uthred of Boldon, a monk of Durham, considered
by many to be the most important Oxford theologian of the
time. More devastating was the crisis that hit England in 1349:
the Black Death. What effect all these worries had on John is not
known, but he may well have considered intercession an important part of a hermit's life.

His meditations begin with a long consideration of Christ cru-
cified, especially of his love to us and the love with which we
should respond to him. Then there are meditations addressed to
the Blessed Virgin Mary, to the Angels, to Abraham and David, to St John the Evangelist, to St Cuthbert. What books John
had with him on the Inner Farne is hard to say. He may have
been drawing on a capacious memory; almost every sentence
has some echo of the Scriptures. He also shows great affection
for the writings of St Bernard, one of the early Cistercian monks
who wrote extensively on the love of God. John's meditations
fit in well with other writings of the fourteenth century, such as
Julian of Norwich and *The Cloud of Unknowing*. Had he written in English, as they did, his work might now be much better
known.

John Whiterig was a happy hermit. One of the most appealing
passages of his book is his description of a vivid vision of Christ.
John in this vision asked Jesus how he could be saved. Jesus'
reply was spoken 'merrily', 'with gaiety and kindness'. He said
to John, 'Love, and thou shalt be saved.' Jesus spoke to him, says
John, 'as though laughing'.

But John believed completely in cheerfulness. It adds so much
to an action, says John. Cheerfulness 'is a sign and an effect of
a loving heart'.

So the Farne Islands give us at least three examples of happy
hermits: first, St Cuthbert, who indeed could weep with those
who weep, but whose cheerfulness was such a marked charac-

teristic that not even the most traditional hagiographer could leave it out; second, Bartholomew of Farne, attracting and enjoying his many visitors; and now, third, John Whiterig.

Nowadays, when I stand on Holy Island and look across the sea to the Inner Farne, I think not only of St Aidan praying against Penda, not only of St Cuthbert fighting the demons, not only of Aethelwald and Felgild with their comforting, healing calfskin, not only of St Bartholomew singing his psalms at the top of his ringing voice, but also of the gentle John Whiterig, to whom our good Lord Jesus said with a broad smile, 'Love, and thou shalt be saved.'

11

From the Reformation to the Outbreak of the Second World War
1537–1939

This chapter covers 400-plus years. The ordinary people of the Island are seen only occasionally in the first 300 years of this time, when they were presumably getting on with fishing, farming and making a living, in varying degrees of poverty. In the last 100 years of this period they become much more visible. Rather than a continuous story we deal here with significant topics, and the first is the building and use of the Castle.

The Castle

For the previous 900 years the dominant building on the Island had been the first or second monastery. During this time the defence of the Island had been either impossible, for example against the Viking raiders, or else in the last resort unnecessary, as against the non-existent Scottish attack. While the Benedictine Priory was in use and partly fortified the aim was to protect people, namely the monks and the villagers, against marauding parties of Scots. But the Castle was built for a different purpose. It is a Tudor construction, not a medieval one, consequently it has no dungeons, torture instruments or suits of armour, and was never inhabited by a baronial family: it is not part of the same group of castles as Bamburgh, Norham, Alnwick, Warkworth, Dunstanburgh and others. Its purpose was to protect the harbour against takeover by any of the King's enemies, especially the Scots. At the time the harbour was much bigger than it is now: big enough to hold a small fleet of royal naval vessels and to land troops and all their equipment and supplies. (Today a visitor who walks from the village towards the Heugh across the field called Sanctuary Close, and diverts a few yards from the path to the left, will see a sudden drop of a few feet in the field. That marks the earlier limit of the sea and will give an idea of the size of the harbour. The visitor may also like to visit the massive Tudor fortifications at Berwick-upon-Tweed, on which much more was spent than on any other military building of the day. Such was the extent of fear of the Scots, in spite of the English victory at Flodden in 1513. Nothing on this scale was built on Holy Island.)

The story of Holy Island Castle is a little uncertain in its early stages. In 1539 the king had ordered that 'all Havens should be fensed with bulwarks and blockehouses against the scots'. In 1542 two bulwarks were constructed, found to be in disrepair by 1544 and repaired. It is not sure where these were, and it is possible that it was intended to defend the area round the priory church for this, with its roof still on, was now a naval storehouse. A certain Robert Rooke 'of Barwick' advised that 'there is stone plentie and sufficient remaining of the old Abbey lately dissolved there', and sometime before 1550 the site of Beblowe Hill was chosen and the Castle built there. But before the completion of the Castle we can see the value of the Island to the English army, for in 1543 the Earl of Hertford had led an expedition to invade the Scottish lowlands, had landed 2,500 troops on the Island and anchored ten warships in the harbour. By 1559 the garrison at the Castle consisted of a non-resident Captain, two master gunners, one master's mate and 20 soldiers. It was to remain at this strength for many years.

The fortifications were maintained in order during Tudor times, but the accession of James VI of Scotland as James I of England formed a union which decreased the military importance of the Castle. One person who should be mentioned at this time, a good example of how important and involved the local gentry were becoming in Tudor times, is Sir William Reed. A soldier, he was connected with the building of Holy Island Castle, was given monastic land at Fenham just across the sea from the Island, built a Manor House there, held the captaincy of Holy Island and the Farnes for life, fought under the Earl of Leicester in Holland at the battle of Zutphen, was knighted there, became a JP in 1594 and in 1603, as an old man, welcomed the new king, James VI & I, to his home at Fenham as the king travelled to London to be crowned. Unfortunately nothing now remains of his manor house at Fenham, but his body lies in Holy Island church.

The Castle re-enters history during the reign of Charles I, the civil war, and with it Captain Rugg, commander of the garrison. A visitor in 1635 had called the Castle a 'dainty little fort' and another, who came with an expedition by Charles I to the north, called it 'a pretty fort'. On this occasion 20 ships anchored in the harbour and two regiments of men were landed. All who met Captain Rugg commented on his great bottle-nose, 'the largest I have ever seen', and on his generous hospitality. But the Captain had his own troubles, among them the fact that he could not get his soldiers' pay from London (which then, perhaps as now, did not believe that Northumberland exists). He wrote several letters to Charles I's advisers and then a letter in verse, which has survived. In it he calls himself 'the greate Commander of the Gormorants', complains 'I owe for bread, beere, beefe in sundry places', wishes 'I wish I had wherewith for to interr me' and asks 'Lett me have what is ordered to be given' and concludes charitably 'And that great God that houlds the Devell in fetters, Blesse good Kinge Charles, myselfe, and you my debtors.' But it seems that he still didn't get his men's pay. So in the Civil War the Castle supported the Parliamentarians, but it seems that they did not pay him either. After he retired and was replaced by a Colonel Shafto, the Parliamentary forces voted for the payment of these arrears and also for the payment of £100 to Captain

Rugg himself. But he died the next year and never received it, nor indeed did the garrison for a further ten years. Shafto was followed by Captain Batton; in 1547, after the Royalists had taken Berwick, he was offered the arrears of pay if he changed to the Royalist side, but honourably he refused. Subsequently the Royalist troops, encamped at Haggerston, cut off all supplies to the Island and the Castle. Relief arrived, but a year later it all happened again; this time Captain Batton's wife managed to get to Newcastle and alert the Parliamentary forces there, and relief and supplies were sent.

Then we hear no more of military threats to the Castle until 1715, the first of the Jacobite rebellions. The famous story has often been told with differing details: this is how it has come to me. One day a little boat with two men in it put into the harbour. By this time the garrison of soldiers was reduced to less than half its original strength, and only two soldiers were actually in the Castle: a master gunner, who made a little extra money by acting as the village barber, and a sentry. The elder man from the boat, Lancelot Errington, came up to the Castle and asked for a shave, or hair-cut, or both. Later in the day he came again with the other man, his nephew Mark, and asked to be allowed in to look for his watch-key, which he thought he had lost there that morning. Once in, the two Erringtons pulled out pistols. One version of the story is that the gunner happened to have a handgrenade beside him which he threw at them, but it failed to explode. The two Jacobites turned the soldiers out of the Castle and ran up the Jacobite flag. However, their signals failed to attract their supporters on the mainland, who failed to come; instead, the garrison of English soldiers came from Berwick and easily captured the Castle and the two men, who eventually escaped. That was the only time in its history that Holy Island Castle actually saw enemy action!

So the years went by, the Castle was in decline, and finally it was demilitarized in 1819. Then it became a coastguard station, then the headquarters of a Volunteer Coast Artillery detachment until 1893, and then was rapidly falling into ruin.

Before leaving the military age we should notice a building which had definitely fallen into ruin, just on the eastern edge of the Heugh. This was built in 1675; it is thought that it was constructed because of the growing threat of Dutch privateers on the east coast at this time. It would have held a small garrison of soldiers and some artillery, presumably to shoot at enemy shipping entering the harbour. But there is no record of its being used and much of it has now been washed away. It is probable that the tide will take it completely, in the end.

For the Castle a new phase began at the end of the nineteenth century and beginning of the twentieth. Edward Hudson, the proprietor of the magazine *Country Life*, acquired the Castle from the Crown, first taking a lease and later purchasing it. He was already friendly with the architect Edwin Lutyens, who was well known as a country-house architect. Hudson asked him to adapt the Castle, basically keeping the Tudor structure but turning it into a gentleman's holiday home. This Lutyens did with great success, giving it an extremely attractive interior and the fairy-tale outline it has when approached from the village.

Lutyens was friendly with Miss Gertrude Jekyll, the foremost garden designer of her time, who had already collaborated with him on many projects. So naturally she was invited to design a garden for the Castle. Since the Castle is placed high on a natural outcrop of rock it was not possible to have a garden very close, though it seems that Edward Hudson toyed with the idea of a water-garden, and indeed when the ground is very soggy after rain or one of our rare falls of snow something like a natural moat forms round the landward side. However, it was decided to use a walled enclosure, which may once had been a sheep pen, some 500 metres north of the Castle, which had the advantage of being visible from all the main rooms.

Miss Jekyll came to the Island in May 1906 'accompanied by Lutyens, a cantankerous raven called Black Jack and a large bag of peppermint bull's eyes' (National Trust *Guide*). She designed within this enclosure a garden of roses, a variety of flowering plants and shrubs, but also herbs and vegetables for use in the kitchen. As it was not expected that the owner would live in the Castle all the year round, the flowers chosen were summer-flowering, when he would be there. The work was done 1911–12.

The garden has now been restored by the National Trust (see Chapter 12).

Edward Hudson entertained some distinguished visitors to the Castle. One in particular was Madame Guilhermina Suggia, a Portuguese cellist. Her evening concerts were normally just for the house party at the Castle, but not always. A lady, now very elderly, remembers as a small child seeing and hearing her. This lady writes:

> Madame Suggia was a very happy and gracious lady. In the evenings she would play for the guests of the house party. On summer evenings the windows of the Ship Room would be open and visitors to the Island used to go and sit among the rocks outside to listen to her playing.
>
> When funds were needed for the war memorial for the first Great War she gave two concerts in the school, one in the afternoon for the visitors and one in the evening for the Island people . . . My mother took my brother and me to the afternoon performance, an experience which I have never forgotten. My mother stood me on one of the window sills so that I would be able to see Madame Suggia playing. My memory is of a beautiful lady, in a wonderful red gown, pouring forth beautiful music. My father pretended to be an Islander and went again in the evening, and said it had been an even more wonderful experience. Madame Suggia said afterwards that she had enjoyed the evening performance even more than the afternoon; she had felt such a response from the Island people and had given encore after encore.

Unfortunately Edward Hudson was not able to continue to maintain the Castle. In 1921 he sold it to Oliver Falk and he, a few years later, to Sir Edward de Stein, whose sister Gladys was frequently resident. They particularly encouraged young members of the family to come for the school holidays and lent it to friends for special family occasions and so on. But in 1944 Sir Edward gave it to the National Trust. He continued as its tenant until he died in 1965, and his sister until she died in 1968.

Industry on Holy Island

The visitor walking today in the northern half of the Island, among the dunes or on the coastal path (the one place to find peace if the village is very busy) may be surprised to know that in the eighteenth and nineteenth centuries there were attempts to establish industry in that area. The present industries are fishing, farming and tourism but, especially in the nineteenth century, it was hoped to exploit coal mining, iron working and lime burning.

Hopes for the first two of these were short-lived. There are coal deposits on the Island and in the 1790s and again in 1840 there were efforts to mine it. But the seams were found to be very thin, 6–24 inches, and mostly at considerable depth. Borings were made in the area of the Snook and Snook House but these were abandoned as unprofitable, and the coal required for lime burning was then imported. Similarly ironstone contained in layers of shale was quarried by an iron company from Falkirk from 1760 until 1794 or thereabouts, but there were considerable difficulties as the ore lay beneath the tide at high water and so the efforts to mine it ceased.

Lime burning was more fortunate for a time. Powdered lime has two main uses: in the building trade for making mortar and in agriculture for neutralizing soils and breaking up heavy clay. Lime burning in a minor way had been practised by the Benedictine monks, but in the nineteenth century two groups of lime kilns were built on the Island.

The earlier of these is known as the Kennedy group. It was situated on the west of the Island to the north of Chare Ends. A wagonway was built to bring the blocks of limestone from the quarry to the kilns. Then it took the powdered lime from the kilns down the west coast past Chare Ends just to the north of a lane called Tripping Chare, where a new jetty had been built for the ships which came to collect it. The remains of these kilns are now almost invisible under the turf and sand.

The second and more successful set of kilns was built close to the Castle (and is now preserved by the National Trust). This venture was undertaken by a lime merchant from Dundee, William Nicholl, who in 1860 built a wagonway from the quarry down the east side of the Island to the Castle Point, where the new kilns were situated, and then another wagonway round the base of the Castle to a new jetty built for the incoming lime-ships. Nicholl owned a number of schooners which sailed into Holy Island harbour laden with coal for the kilns and took the powdered lime back to Dundee. At first this must have seemed likely to succeed. In 1851 only seven labourers and a blacksmith were employed in the lime industry, but by 1861 this had risen to 30 labourers (many of whom were Scottish), an engine smith and two blacksmiths. In the 1871 census the number of employees was 24, but in the 1881 list there were only eight. The enterprise did not succeed long term. Nicholl never took his full quota of 5,000 tons of limestone annually and the number of visits by his schooners gradually dropped. After about 1883 it appears that the kilns were not used; Mr. Nicholl drops out of the picture and it seems that the kilns were fired for the last time in 1900 for lime for the Island farmers.

Today the visitor can easily follow the line of the wagonway, though the rails and sleepers (if there were any) have disappeared. The wagons were drawn by horses, except for one tantalizing reference to a steam-engine: it could be that this was a mistake. Such details of the shape of the wagons are not known.

One more attempt was made to improve the Island's industrial potential, this time with the fishing industry in mind. The Lord of the Manor in 1903 was Major L. Morley Crossman. In order to make it easier for fishermen to sell their catch on the mainland he proposed that a branch railway line should be built, connecting with the existing North Eastern Railway just north of Beal, at Goswick. A similar plan at Seahouses had been brought into operation, but of course for the Island the crossing of the sands had to be negotiated. Major Crossman's plan included the re-opening of the lime kilns, the reconstruction of the jetty for fishing boats, and a line crossing the sands on an elevated pier supported on piles, to go across the Castle Field to the kilns and then on to the jetty. He consulted both the Lord Lieutenant and the General Manager of the North Eastern Railway but both were discouraging and the plan was abandoned. Among those who were relieved at this outcome was Edward Hudson, who had feared it would spoil his plan for the Castle.

And so the Island returned to its own way of farming, fishing and peace; and turned increasingly to welcoming the tourists.

A royal visit

Among the 'tourists' we must mention members of the Royal Family, who have paid three visits to the Island in the last hundred years, in 1908, 1958 and 2008. (See Chapter 12 for the second and third.) The first visit was of the then Prince and Princess of Wales, later to be George V and Queen Mary, who were visiting the Duke of Northumberland at Alnwick Castle. The visit was on 2 July.

A guidebook to the island, dated 1909, described it as follows:

> As the Royal party drove into the market square they were received by weather-beaten jersey-clad fishermen on one side of the road and by the school children on the other. It was a picturesque scene with the newly whitewashed, red-tiled cottages in the background and the sea in the distance, placidly simmering under the glorious sunshine. After the presentation of a bouquet by the children and a pretty shell basket by the older people their Royal Highnesses entered the ground of the Manor House, where they planted two sycamore trees, one on

each side of a privet bush which was planted about ten years ago by the late Duchess of Teck. They then examined the ruins of the priory . . .

They also visited the Castle on this occasion, and some account of this is preserved in a letter from Lutyens to his wife. He did not think the visit was a total success. Apparently Hudson was rigid with nerves; the Prince thought the way up to the Castle door was alarming and was also worried about the rising tide; the Princess disliked the cobbles which hurt her feet; the Duke of Northumberland and other members of the party were politely bored.

But if the principal guests were a little bored and uncomfortable the Islanders certainly were not. They were having a real day's holiday. Old family photographs show the women and the girls beautifully attired in long summer dresses. There were flags flying from the yachts in the harbour, there were games for the schoolchildren, a football match and at night a bonfire on the Heugh. When the royal carriage was about to depart the people gathered round to wave good-bye, and the last thing the Prince and Princess saw of Holy Island was a banner on the last refuge box saying COME AGAIN. As far as we know they didn't.

Church life

The parish church of St Mary the Virgin stands, we believe, on the site of St Aidan's first wooden church. Still within the Anglo-Saxon years this was replaced by a small stone church on the same spot. This little church became the parish church when the Benedictine Priory was established. Had the Benedictines not found a church standing which could be adapted to serve the parish they would have built one, for their monasteries were intended to be enclosed and so the monastic church was not available for ordinary parish purposes. (There are many examples of this elsewhere in England, where a small parish church stands next to the Benedictine ruin which founded it and which it has outlived.) So this was the church for the villagers. The Priory appointed the priest and paid him.

This church was enlarged in stages: from 1150 the north aisle and its arcade, romanesque style, were erected; an arch was made in the earlier solid east wall and a Norman apse was built. The round chancel arch of this period can still be seen in the wall. Around a hundred years later, about 1250, the south aisle and its arcade were built, the Norman apse was demolished and the present chancel was erected. We do not know whether the need was for more space for people, or for the satisfaction of building in the new Early English (early Gothic) style with its pointed arches. A little later the north and south walls were re-built further out to allow broader aisles. The windows of the north wall show the very beginning of the decorated style: three windows in one. But there development stopped. So the body of the church existed by 1300; the porches were added later and the bellcote not until 1723. Burial for parishioners would have been in the churchyard.

Before the Reformation the interest is focused on the monastery and we hear hardly anything about these parishioners. After the Reformation, and after the religious situation had settled and the Anglican church had emerged, we suppose that most people on the Island were Anglicans. A vicar now replaced the priests previously provided for the parish church by the priory. We have a complete list of vicars up to the present day, but most of them are simply names on a list. A few may surprise us with their length of tenure: in the eighteenth century a father and son divided 74 years between them: James Robertson senior was Vicar from 1716 to 1738, and James Robertson junior from 1738 to 1790. My imagination refused to comment.

But the church fell into a bad state of repair. We get glimpses of it over the next centuries. In 1646 Thomas Shaftoe, Captain of the Castle, gave black oak pews and an oak pulpit. But it seems that by the eighteenth century things were as bad again or worse: the chancel was partly roofless and part boarded off to form the vestry; the eastern half of the nave was boarded off and used for services. The mid nineteenth century saw drastic repair work. The church was completely cleared and the floor of the nave was levelled. Pews for the nave of pitchpine were provided and a new pine pulpit. (The vicar of the time, Mr. Keeling, discovered pieces of the old black oak pulpit thrown out; he rescued them to make the present lectern, which is therefore the oldest wood in the church.) The Ecclesiastical Commissioners restored the chancel. The north porch had served as a mortuary for bodies recovered from the sea, its door on to the churchyard had been opened and its other door into the church had been blocked. This was now reversed and the porch became the vestry. Finally the whole of the interior walls of the nave were covered in lath and plaster. This work of restoration was completed in 1860. So there was a clean and decent church; it must have seemed an enormous improvement.

Meanwhile another development in church life was the growth of Presbyterianism on the Island. This had developed in Scotland and there were normally a number of Scottish Presbyterians living on the Island. In 1793 just 11 of the 80 families on the Island were Presbyterian, and it seems that they were happy enough to attend the Anglican church.

That situation began to change in 1832. For some reason a Mr Buchan of Kelloe encouraged a young Presbyterian probationer to see Holy Island as a sphere for mission: his name was Alexander Moody and he worked here for three years. He conducted evening services in the schoolhouse and began a Sunday School. In November 1834 a cholera epidemic struck the Island, apparently from a foreign ship in the harbour. Mr Moody worked courageously and continuously in visiting the sick and won great respect for this work. But in 1835 he left the Island to work elsewhere, and his efforts were not followed up.

However, in 1860 the United Presbyterian Church of Scotland 'adopted' the Island as a preaching station. A building was rented for their meetings and by 1872 they had grown to 29 members. A cottage opposite the Lindisfarne Hotel was next used, but when that became too small it was decided to build a church. Sir

William Crossman (Lord of the Manor) donated the land and a fund raised the required money for building. The church was opened on 19 May 1892 and dedicated to St Cuthbert. In 1876 it had become part of the newly formed Presbyterian Church of England but it was not possible to appoint a regular minister to the church because of lack of funds and accommodation.

In 1932 a centenary celebration was held: 100 years since Alexander Moody. There was a fairly small but faithful congregation, but the church was still served by retired ministers or students. This was the situation at the beginning of the Second World War.

Education

The first definite information we have about the provision for a school for the people of Holy Island dates from the Bill of Enclosure of 1793. Land was set aside for a school with a schoolhouse for the master. It was built in 1796 by subscription from various local worthies. It seems from records that this was the only school on the Island: other places had 'Dame's schools' or 'charity schools' but we have no evidence of these here.

In 1796, of course, education was neither compulsory nor free. It cost a few pence per week. For a number of reasons education for some children was erratic: their families could afford the fees one week but not the next, or they were needed to work on the farms, or they were suffering from one or other of the childhood illnesses which naturally spread very easily in such a close community. Numbers varied greatly. In 1796 the school opened with 18 children; by the 1850s there were 40-plus; some old Islanders only recently departed told me they could remember the schoolroom with 80 pupils.

An important name is William Markwell. He was born here in 1828, left home and eventually became a prosperous ship-owner in Devon, but did not forget the Island. After his death, and that of his wife, by the terms of his will a Holy Island Charity was set up and trustees appointed to provide education at the island school first for his relatives and their descendants and then for as many poor children as the money would stretch to. (When school fees were abolished this income became an endowment for Holy Island School.) He also endowed what is still known as the Markwell Sermon, to be preached by the Vicar on the second Sunday in August on the subject of education. For this the Vicar was to be paid two guineas!

The Education Act of 1870 made schooling compulsory but still not free; there must have been families on the Island who could not afford it, but also there was no one to enforce the Act. In 1880 children were expected to stay at school until they reached ten years; by 1918 this had become 14 years; by 1944 15 years. The Island School continued to take pupils of all ages up to 1966.

The First World War, 1914–18

The visitor who now goes up on to the Heugh and studies the War Memorial will see that the Island lost eight men in the First World War and three in the Second. This is the general pattern across the country: many more members of the Armed Forces were killed in the first war than in the second. But to say that the Island lost eight is not to convey any true idea of the extent of Island involvement. In fact 67 men fought in the first war: 25 in the Navy, of whom two were killed, and 42 in the Army, with the loss of six. The Roll of Honour for this war is kept in St Mary's church and shows that, in addition to these eight, 19 Island men were wounded. This list also shows the extent of the contribution of certain families: six Wilsons 'joined up', six Walkers, five Cromartys, four Markwells, four Darlings. Many other families sent two or three, and of the families who sent just one we remember that he could have been their only one. So apart from the sacrifice by the men who went, we should consider the sacrifice by the wives, mothers, grandparents and other family members who stayed at home.

Nowadays on Remembrance Sunday we begin our service in church and include the two minutes' silence and solemn reading of the names of those who died in both wars. We then process up to the War Memorial on the Heugh, to read the names again and lay wreathes. In addition to these we should remember those who went out and returned; those who came back wounded, those for whom life could never be the same again. It seems a magnificent contribution for a small Island.

The lifeboats of Holy Island

The story of the Holy Island lifeboats is one of heroism and success. The heroism no one can doubt once they are aware of the hidden rocks and currents and have experienced, even while safely on land, the strength of some of our hurricanes and the threatening roaring of the sea ('calling for its next victim', as people used to say). The success is shown by the fact that since 1865, when the RNLI took over the management of the lifeboats and records are available, there have been 205 launches and 336 lives saved, and no lifeboat-man's life has been lost, though there was one very narrow escape. We can look back on it now as a completed chapter, as the Island no longer has a lifeboat. It was decided that, in these days of much faster boats and better technology, and indeed of fewer ships and boats out there, the lifeboats at Seahouses and Berwick were sufficient.

The Island's first two lifeboats were not named. They were given by the Lord Crewe Trustees in 1789 and 1829 and were kept by the Castle. When the RNLI was established here three lifeboat stations were eventually built. The first, on the beach just opposite St Cuthbert's Island, has survived as a complete building. The second was on the north side of the Island near the Snook; some remains of it may be seen. It had replaced an unsuccessful attempt to house one at Ross Links. The third was under the Heugh and had a ramp from the boathouse directly into the deep water. This helped to solve the difficult problem of how the boats were to be launched. Launching had sometimes needed horses to pull the boat across land to the nearest point to the 'casualty' in the sea. Then the boat had to be pushed right out into the sea. The women often took part in this, wading right up to their waists in bitterly cold sea-water. Once the women of the Island received a RNLI award for doing this.

The lifeboats were named *Grace Darling* (1 and 2), *Bombay, Bedford, Edward and Eliza, Lizzie Porter, Milburn, Gertrude.* The *Grace Darlings* together were responsible for 118 lives saved but the individual record was held by the *Lizzie Porter*, having saved 77 lives. She was the last of the rowing-boats and seems to be the one most affectionately remembered. The *Milburn*, the first of the motor-boats, had saved 44 lives by December 1939.

Of course there are stories about particular excursions. Sometimes scratch crews were necessary. On two occasions the vicars took out a crew. The Revd W. W. F. Keeling did this in 1892, and in 1896 the Revd David Bryson, knowing that a fishing boat was in distress and could not get in across the bar, got volunteers (who included the sexton, the publican of the Northumberland Arms, a fish merchant, two sick fishermen and others), took the *Grace Darling* and brought the fishing boat safely in. Of course, in very many cases when the lifeboat was launched, it was not to save lives known to be at risk but to stand by the fishing fleet in bad weather and escort the boats in. The interested visitor may study the boards on the wall opposite the Priory Museum, for the list of launches and the reason in each case.

Among the men it was considered a great honour to get a place in the lifeboat, and so when the signal was sounded all who could do so ran to the boat to be among the first there. One wife told me that once when the signal was heard her husband had not got his boots on, but he ran all the same and she ran after him carrying his boots! Miss Elfreda Elford, now 93 years old, whose father was Vicar in 1937, described to me a day when the boat was called out in snow and very heavy seas. People on land lost sight of her altogether; in fact, in one terrific swell she completely overturned but amazingly managed to right herself with all the men in place except the coxswain, who had been washed out of his seat although his clothing caught in part of the gear and he was saved. Next morning on the Island, which was Sunday, the church was packed but the atmosphere was very tense. Then the boat was seen returning. She had managed to get into Seahouses, had rested there and then come safely back. Elfreda told me that, as each man got out of the boat, his wife went to him and they went up to their house in silence. Then the great rejoicing.

On that occasion, and no doubt on others, there was in fact no 'casualty': there had been a mistake in calling the boat. Had our lifeboat and all its lives been lost the tragedy would have underlined the risks the men took and the generosity of their willingness to continue to answer the call.

The lifeboat story continues for just a little while after 1939 (see Chapter 12).

Fishing and salvaging

Through these centuries fishing was the major occupation of the Island men. Mostly they are invisible in the records. But Mr Ralph Wilson, who is himself a fisherman, has allowed us to see extracts from a diary kept by his grandfather John Wilson who was fishing here at the turn of the nineteenth and twentieth centuries.

John mentions that his boat held five men who shared out equally the profits of their work. He notes their catch as haddock, codling, plaice, crabs and herring, which was frequently the main catch. Interestingly, in the extracts I have seen, he does not mention lobster. Occasionally he quotes the price that the fishermen received for their catch:

1899 crabs 2 shillings (modern 10 pence) for 20
codling 1 shilling and sixpence (7.5p) a stone
haddock 1 shilling and sixpence (7.5p) a stone
plaice 5 shillings and sixpence (30p) a stone

In 1901 he mentions that the men in his boat got only £10.6s each for a three-month season. There were very few herrings, he says, and very poor prices.

He mentions several storms, too strong for the fishing boats. It was a hard life. The fishermen were glad to supplement their income by the salvage money they received for helping to recover ships from the rocks or the sands. It is clear from John's diary that there were many more of these than the books mention: often quite small boats in need of a helping hand.

But in the decades to follow bigger wrecks occurred in these rocky and dangerous waters. Sometimes, when the lifeboat had rescued the crews of these stricken vessels, the ship itself would be lost. This happened, for example, to the aged coaster *Locksley*, which in 1938 hit the rocks just off the *False* Emmanuel Head (a rocky ridge running out north of Sandham Bay). The crew was rescued in a particularly difficult operation but the vessel sank.

But sometimes a large number of the Island people were involved in a salvage operation. Two examples occur just at the beginning of the Second World War. In 1939 the Norwegian cargo ship *Royal* ran on to the sands in thick fog and in 1940 the Danish steamer *Prins Kund*, again in fog, ran aground on the north side of the Island. In both cases the method of salvage was effective: the Island people dug a channel in the sand and, at every tide, eased the ship by degrees until she could be refloated. In both cases this took six weeks of work, the Islanders sometimes digging by moonlight. Of course the people received salvage dues, as was right.

There are other wrecks which live in the memory of the present Island people. In 1916 the *Cydonia* ran aground on False Emmanuel Head. Her crew was rescued by the *Lizzie Porter* but her cargo of coal was lost with the ship. Island tradition speaks of a large amount of coal being washed up on to Coves Bay. It still happens now, but in quite small chunks. In 1941 the *Coryton* was wrecked just south of the Island. She was loaded with grain (the seagulls had a feast) but as she was in shallow water a lot of the ship was salvaged.

In the last half century these wrecks have become a thing of the past. Occasionally we see ships passing by on the horizon, but they keep quite clear of our rocky waters. But very many wrecks, or parts of wrecks, still lie in the waters around the Island. Now they are of most interest to those practising the modern sport of diving, who occasionally discover something not previously known.

12

From 1939 to the Present Day

The Island in wartime

In 1939 the population of the Island was 220. At he outbreak
of the war 38 young men joined the Forces immediately, and the
number rose to 60 by 1944. Some families had as many as four
or five sons away. Of these men three never returned: two died
serving in the Navy, and one in the Army.

The feel of the Island during the war can be conveyed by a
number of incidents. One of these happened at the very beginning. A lady, now of advanced years, told me that she and her
mother received an invitation to a tea-party given by the three
Misses Davis on the Island. The theme of this party was 'the
women of England must keep up their morale'. All the ladies invited (no men) were told to come in their most colourful dresses,
hats(!) and jewellery. So one lady arrived in what she had recently worn to a wedding: 'a very large hat trimmed with flowers
and veiling, a 1930s dress in floral chiffon, all frills and flowing
scarves'. Another came wearing the family heirloom, which was
a choker necklace of pearls. They had a lovely time. The lady
who told me about it said: 'In the dark days that followed my
thoughts often went back to the colour and gentle companion-
ship of that party. It was like a pebble dropped in a pool and
spreading ripples far and wide.'

But the days that followed were indeed very dark, as the
Island with the rest of the country went into 'blackout'. The first

winters of the war were severe. In those early years when invasion was a real possibility it was thought that the Island might be a point for the landing of enemy tanks. So concrete blocks were provided (they can be seen now at the mainland end of the causeway) to hinder the progress of tanks across the sands (no causeway yet) and give further time and warning. The Islanders had to take turns to be 'coast-watchers'. The two points from which the coast-watchers peered into the darkness across the sea were the Castle and an old car parked on the cliffs at Coves Bay on the north shore. A lady who remembers this car describes it: 'They made it very comfortable, packing it around with sods of grass and earth, leaving only the door and the window showing. It must have been almost invisible from the air.' The naturalist Richard Perry, who was living on the Island then, writes of a terrifying moment when he was on coast-watch in this car, on a snowy and totally black winter's night. He was feeling quite drowsy when suddenly he heard, out of the blackness, 'a tortured screaming, surely that of a child'. He managed to get the car open, semi-paralysed as he was with fear. The scream came again. Then he relaxed, got back into the car, laughing at himself, for he was a naturalist and should have known. The Island has foxes; they mate in winter and 'that tortured child's screaming out in the darkness was the dreadful love-howl of the vixen!' But not a nice experience in those circumstances.

As far as I know the coast-watchers never detected any enemy action. But on 5 November 1941 a little boat with five young men in it arrived on the Island. They were from Kristiansand in Norway and they had escaped across the North Sea to join the Allied forces against Hitler, as many Norwegians sought to do. Very recently here we received a letter from the niece of one of them. His name was Sven Moe and the letter described in detail how, with four others, all of them 19 or 20 years old, he stole his father's boat (it was essential for his father not to know in advance, in case of German reprisals), stole fuel for it from the Germans at the airport, and set out on 1 November. On the crossing they were all very sea-sick; they had to travel in the dark without any lights; they had to avoid mines of which the seas were full; and they completely lost their way. When they sighted land they saw a strange castle, houses . . . but hardly cared any longer because they were so tired. They landed. Someone shouted, 'Friend or foe?' It was England; it was in fact Holy Island. They got a splendid reception, breakfast at the Lindisfarne Hotel, lots of cigarettes, lots of welcome. When they were sent on to London a message from there was sent to the underground (resistance) movement in Kristiansand in code: 'five boxes of cowberry arrived'. Their boat was sold and the money put on account for Sven's father.

They joined the Forces and were sent to Canada. Sadly four of them died in the war. Sven's niece got the details of the story from the one who survived, Kay Thorsen.

Another incident which brought the war home to the people of Holy Island was on 7 May 1941 when a German Junkers bomber came down on the Island. It had been on a bombing raid over Glasgow, had been attacked by British fighter planes and had lost one engine. The crew were hoping to limp home across the sea but when they reached the east coast they realized they could not make it. When they saw a wide, sandy beach (the North Shore) they landed safely on it. They managed to set fire to their plane, but it was not completely burned, and afterwards bits of it were sought after as souvenirs by the Island children. Then the German airmen were taken prisoner by our own homeguard and coastguard, were taken to Berwick by the police and from there sent to a prisoner of war camp in Canada. I am told that this incident gave the schoolmaster of the time an unexpected opportunity to practise his German!

Of course all the deprivations of the war years were felt on the Island: the rationing, the darkness, the news bulletins that concealed the real news, and especially the anxiety about the men who were away. The Island of course had a homeguard. The older men and the boys not yet old enough to enlist put on uniform, drilled, were equipped with rifles and practised with them on the beach. They were not called upon to use them in earnest, but the fame of our homeguard spread abroad: on 1 July 1942 the *Yorkshire Post* had a headline: 'Lindisfarne is Alert'. But one man, who spent part of a recovery leave here and wrote about it, found that the Island still had more peace, more beauty and more friendliness than he had known elsewhere.

So the war years ended. The men returned, to resume their old lives or make new lives for themselves. But to three families these years had brought tragedy, for Adam Shell Henderson, Thomas Walker and George Cromarty Douglas did not come home.

The growth of tourism

Probably the most noticeable development in the decades since the war has been the enormous growth in the number of visitors. This has been made possible by the building first of the bridge over the Low, that stream of water from the mainland which cuts its way through the sand, and second by the causeway, so that it is now possible to drive, at low tide, directly on to the Island. So people come and, particularly if there is a combination of three things – a good tide (one that is open for the middle part of the day), good weather and a Bank Holiday – they come in thousands, mostly just for the day, a few for the weekend or longer.

They come for a number of different reasons, not all connected with the 'holiness' of the Island. For the historically minded there are the historic buildings: the parish church, the Priory, the Castle. Some visitors like to wander in the rather attractive little village; others make for the rocks, the sea, the beaches. It is an official Area of Outstanding Natural Beauty. Some come to pore over the tombstones and trace their ancestry, since there has been such a recent growth in family history. The bird-life is easier to study in winter than in summer, but is abundant in both: I understand that the Island is one of the best places to study the migrations, and that is when we are most visited by ornithologists. We have some remarkable flowers in the dunes in summer, including one orchid which is our very own and grows nowhere else in the world. And I have been surprised, particularly if I have been trying to cross the causeway as the tide approaches, especially on a Sunday, to see how many people come to the mainland edge of the causeway just to see the water cross the road.

The pilgrims

Among the visitors a large and growing group are the pilgrims, whose main interest is in the Christian past-and-present of the Island. These are very varied. I am always intrigued by those who come to the Island and hate it. I don't mean simply that they don't particularly like it or find it boring. I mean they absolutely hate it. They find the feel of it oppressive; they can't breathe; they enter the church and bolt out again, because they feel attacked. Clearly these people are sensitive to something here, and it is not for them.

Then there are those who come and are disappointed because it is not Iona; they are balanced of course by those who are glad it is not Iona. There are those who are surprised, even not pleased, to find that there is an ordinary working village here; they had thought it was just a rock, with maybe a church and a ruined priory, in the middle of the sea. More interesting are those who find something they like even if they can't find the right words to express it; they say the Island has 'something special'. Others may use a more religious vocabulary: they say 'God is here' or that they can pray here. Some have had religious experiences here which have changed their lives. I think of one man who makes a personal pilgrimage once a year because about 30 years ago he had an experience on the Island which brought his faith alive, and he returns every year to thank God. There are probably many such individual pilgrimages, most of which are cherished and kept private.

Bigger pilgrimages can vary enormously. The biggest I ever saw was one for our own diocese, Newcastle, celebrating the centenary of Independence (formerly we were part of Durham diocese). That was about 6,000 people; mercifully the weather was good, but the pilgrimage service was held out in the Castle Field as the organizers did not think it could be fitted into the Priory.

It is of course very natural for people of the North-East to come back to what they consider their own Christian home, their 'cradle of Christianity'. There are other diocesan pilgrimages, especially if there is some sense of connection. For example, the diocese of Chichester came to us, because they look on St Wilfrid as their founding apostle and he was originally one of ours. The diocese of Truro came, only 40 of them, but still a long way from home and with no known connections with the Lindisfarne tradition. Smaller pilgrimages are legion. We have parish and deanery pilgrimages from many parts of the country, and some for special groups such as the Mothers' Union. Big pilgrimages must hold their services in the open air, usually in the Priory ruins. Smaller ones usually book the parish church. I have known as many as six pilgrimage groups, all wanting their own service in the church, in one afternoon. Such groups quite often add to their programme by asking us for a talk about the saints or the Island history; this talk would normally happen in the parish church, a largish building with its roof still on!

The parish church post-war

When the restoration was completed in 1860 (see Chapter 11) the church was in a sound, clean and usable condition and no further work was done on the structure. However, in the last 40 years most of the lath and plaster which the Victorians had used to cover the interior walls of the nave has been removed, so uncovering the beauty of the natural many-coloured sandstone and also revealing a number of architectural details which had been concealed. For example, the 'Saxon door' high in the wall above the chancel arch had been completely concealed, as had the marks on the south wall which indicate the remodelling of the original windows. So we could grasp more of the history of the church as a building, and there may be more to discover when the last of the plaster, above the two set of arches, is removed.

The most recent work in the church has been the construction immediately inside the main door of a stone ramp, essential for wheelchairs but also, we think, a thing of beauty in itself. Next to it two new sets of shallow steps with elegant iron rails make a much safer entrance for everyone. (I watched with incredulity the first visitor who actually fell down them, fortunately not damaging himself.) Further modifications of the church are at the planning stage. Outside in the churchyard the paths have been widened and surfaced and lamps have been provided, very welcome on winter evenings in what was the darkest corner of the village.

Visitors entering St Mary's just to look round will now find much of beauty and interest. First to catch their eye will be the statue by the sculptor Fenwick Lawson called 'The Journey'. This shows six monks, a little more than lifesize, carrying an open coffin on which rests the body of St Cuthbert. They are on their way to Durham (see Chapter 10). The varied, sensitive faces of the monks speak of courage, persistence, loyalty, community and remind us of all the best features of those monastic centuries. The other piece of sculpture in the church is the font cover, a figure of a baby with the dove of the Holy Spirit. This is by the sculptor Kathleen Parbury, who also made the statue of St Aidan in the churchyard. The work of earlier Island wood-carvers is remembered in the replica of the coffin of St Cuthbert showing the seventh-century carving of angels and saints: this is against the wall in the north aisle. The original is in the Treasury of Durham Cathedral.

Two handmade carpets lie in front of the two altars, both based on designs in the Lindisfarne Gospels. The one in front of the main altar copies the St Mark 'carpet-page'; this was made by Island women and placed there in 1970. In front of St Peter's altar is St Luke's carpet-page, also made by Island women and placed there to celebrate the millennium. The making of new hassocks is an ongoing project, masterminded by one of our churchwardens. We have four handmade chasubles of the colours of the four seasons of the Church's year: green, gold, red and purple. These were made for us by two members of the Durham Cathedral Guild of Broderers and are worn by the priest presiding at the Eucharist.

From a slightly earlier age the church has stained-glass windows, though none from the medieval period. Most of them are from the nineteenth century and include the brilliantly coloured Ascension window in the east. In the west wall are two twentieth-century windows, depicting St Aidan and St Cuthbert, designed by Leonard Evetts. The hatchments hanging in the chancel are coats-of-arms painted on the death of a member of a prominent local family, hung for a while in the house of the deceased, then brought into church. These are of the families of Askew, Haggerston (two) and Selby.

So there is plenty of colour and interest for the visitor to see, and in addition there are the things which change: the flower arrangements looked after lovingly by a member of the congregation, and the various information stands. For we emphasize that this is not a museum but a working, worshipping church. We love and value our past, but we do not live in it. Six days a week there are the three Anglican services of Morning Prayer, Eucharist and Evening Prayer, and for these we always get a congregation, sometimes as many as 30 people. On Sundays there are two Eucharists and Evening Prayer. This pattern is maintained throughout the year, 21 services a week, and most of the congregation will be visitors. In addition there are the needs of the parish, including baptisms, weddings, funerals. In addition we provide whatever is required by the groups of visitors who wish to use the church for special services. We also have the occasional concerts and school events.

The visitors who really surprise us are those who clearly think Christian worship died many years ago, and who ask, 'How long is it since this church was last in use for a service?' We look at our watches to answer that one!

The United Reformed Church/St Cuthbert's Centre

In 1972 our Presbyterian Church became part of the United Reformed Church when the Congregational Union and the Presbyterian Church of England united. By the 1980s the small and now elderly congregation had Sunday evening services led by visiting clergy, but it was clear this could not continue. In the 1990s the last member and elder of the church died. The District Council of the URC, after wider consultation, decided on a new project. The Revd Barry Hutchinson, the second and present Director of this, describes its purpose, inspired by what is known of St Cuthbert: 'The new ministry would encourage the practice of solitude, promote Christian teaching, facilitate the renewal of worship styles and content . . . work towards individual and community reconciliation with the self, other and God . . . all of this within the underpinning context of a warm Christian, welcoming hospitality.' The first Director, the Revd Ian Fosten, who stayed for four years, was the pioneer in the total re-development of the church building and garden and the growth of a ministry to local people, visitors and pilgrims. In the year 2000, under the second Director the name was changed to 'St Cuthbert's Centre'. He continues to explain what is offered:

> Material developments have included the installation of new kitchen facilities and upgrading of the single accommodation known as the Bothy, a quiet retreat and shelter for the many retreatants and pilgrims from around the world who stay there. Along with individuals many church groups hire the Centre for quiet days and longer periods of retreat . . .

The Director is available to lead retreats and provide facilities for such groups and individuals. Morning prayer is held at the Centre on most weekdays, and on Saturday evenings an experience of worship 'perhaps increasingly quiet and gently reflective but nevertheless challenging, comforting and inspiring . . . Communion is celebrated once a month. High days and holidays,

such as St Cuthbert's Day and Christmas, are celebrated in style
. . . usually ending in a party atmosphere as people celebrate the
goodness of God.'

The Centre is open daily and from time to time hosts various displays. August has become the month for art exhibitions
'which attract thousands of people to see and participate in the
current explosion of Christian creativity'. Less obvious is the
little chapel, the old boiler house, open all the time as a place for
individual quiet and shelter. Ecumenical relations are good: the
Centre 'seeks always to co-operate with other Christian groups
and participates, for example, in the seasonal weekly healing
services which travel around the island's three churches. All
people of faith or no faith are welcome . . .'

There are further plans for development both inside and outside
the building, and also beyond the Island. The Director writes:

> Nationally, the United Reformed Church has no centre spe-
> cifically for the promotion of and research into Reformed
> spirituality, and St Cuthbert's is well suited to be part of any
> future development in that area of our church's life, which
> is lately more confident and energetic than it has been for a
> number of years. . . . the United Reformed Church has good
> grounds to be increasingly confident that St Cuthbert's Centre
> will continue to be part of a newly re-vitalized Church life
> and mission.

I think that anyone who remembers the church as it was (as I do)
and goes into it now for the first time will simply stand amazed:
it has become an immensely attractive environment for its varied
uses and for the large number of people who enter and enjoy it.

The Roman Catholic Church

The Roman Catholic Church had one or two families on the
Island in the eighteenth and nineteenth centuries and, from the
late nineteenth century, visited the Island in pilgrimage groups.

But since the Second World War a more permanent presence has been established. There are currently about nine Roman Catholic adults living on the Island and five children. Father Tony Owens, who is Parish Priest at Seahouses and here, describes the recent developments:

It is part of a long tradition that those who aspire 'to be a pilgrim' should cut themselves off for some time from the normal round of daily life. We are blessed to have within our diocese and country a place of pilgrimage, a sacred and cherished Holy Island of Lindisfarne, and, on its Green Lane, St Aidan's: our refurbished church and visitors' centre.

The Roman Catholic presence was first established in Lindisfarne House on Green Lane by Fr J. Corrigan (Lowick). One of its rooms served as a Chapel (15 people) for some time. On 10 November 1957 he launched an appeal to fund the extension, which would be used as a Hall, Dining area and Chapel.

The presence developed because of the new causeway access. The number of pilgrims grew and many children rejoiced in spending a holiday in the adjoining camp organized and funded by the Diocesan Society of St Vincent de Paul.

Bishop Kevin Dunn, ordained Bishop of Hexham and Newcastle on 25 May 2004, referred to Holy Island as 'the Heart of the Diocese' and immediately inspired a complete update and refurbishment of St Aidan's. He appointed Fr Tony Owens Parish Priest of St Aidan's in September 2005 and work began.

The new church and visitors' centre was blessed and opened by Bishop Kevin Dunn on Easter Day, 8 April 2007. Sister Tessa Fisk, Daughter of the Cross of Liege, is Pastoral Assistant, resides on the Island and attends daily to the needs of pilgrims and visitors.

The first season ended with a visit, offering of mass and the blessing of St Aidan's, by the Papal Nuncio, Archbishop Faustino Sainz-Munoz on 20 October 2007.

We have countless pilgrims and visitors who call in to reflect and pray – a powerful legacy of Bishop Kevin Dunn's vision. Sadly and unexpectedly he died on 1 March 2008. 'Pilgrimage accomplished'. May he rest in Peace. Amen.

So all three churches on the Island are alive and lively. In the last half-century three further Christian initiatives have been undertaken, two of them centred on the Island and the third with strong Island connections.

Marygate House

Marygate House as a Christian centre was founded in 1969 by the then vicar, Revd Denis Bill and Mr Douglas Graham, a teacher and Methodist lay preacher. They wanted a 'place where Christians could meet'. When the house became available a trust was quickly formed and Miss Joan Harris joined the team. Douglas and Joan became the first two joint-wardens and the house opened at Easter 1970.

Since then the property has increased by the gradual acquisition of Elemore cottage next door and Cambridge House (on lease) with its three cottages. The number of guests gradually built up to about 1,200 a year. The Trust Deed had made it clear from the start that it was not to cater for seaside holidays, but for groups and individuals who came to the Island with an appropriate religious, educational or cultural programme.

The guests are looked after by a warden and team members. The present warden, Ian Mills, writes of the features of Marygate House that are most important to him.

It is an ecumenical house, welcoming people of all traditions, seeking to serve them, imposing nothing, without even a fixed charge for staying here. It is important to me that our door is never closed on people for lack of money. Donations are welcomed but never required, and no one is made to feel awkward about this.

It is important to me that the House operates with respect to the Island community, in no way threatening the community's traditions and beliefs, but as part of that community joining in with Island activities as much as we can.

The groups who come are immensely varied. Under the heading 'religious' we receive Anglican parishes, Baptists, Methodists, Russian Orthodox and recently a group of Christians and Muslims in dialogue. Vocations conferences and ordinands' weekends are welcomed. The 'educational' slot is filled with primary and secondary school groups, including Roman Catholic schools, and many varied groups of university students. Under 'cultural' there are musical groups, calligraphers, bird watchers, other artists, Myers-Briggs weekends.

The lease on Cambridge House enables us to offer quiet facilities for individual retreats, individual study time, clergy sabbaticals and those essential commodities, space and time, for all under stress and in need of them.

Guests come from many parts of the world: America, Australia, Finland, Norway, Ireland, Wales, Scotland and all over England, with a good number from our own North-East.

The best thing is that they keep coming back.

The Community of Aidan and Hilda

The founder of this community, the Revd Ray Simpson, now the International Guardian, came to live on this Island in 1994, in the cottage he named 'Lindisfarne Retreat'. He had already begun discussions with others about the possibility of a community, and ideas developed over some time. In 1998/9 the house now known as the 'Open Gate' was acquired as the central house of the community. Ray explains its origin and ideals as follows:

The Community of Aidan and Hilda is an international body of Christians who journey with God, and seek to reconnect with the Spirit and the Scriptures, the saints and the streets,

153

the seasons and the soil to heal a wounded world. Its Catholic, Orthodox and Protestant members take vows to follow a Way of Life based on a rhythm of prayer and work, study and re-creation, care for creation and people. Each shares their journey with a spiritual companion known as a soul friend. They chose Aidan as a symbol of a gentle, unthreatening but prophetic Christian who lays down his life for another people, and Hilda as a symbol of a nurturer of the gifts of all, who crosses the divide between different frameworks. The two together are a sign of different genders and races working together for the common good. The Community has over two hundred members in Europe, North America, Africa and Oceania, plus Friends and the occasional linked house or church, and provides worship and educational resources for a renewal of church life.

The Community's founders had links with Lindisfarne, starting in the 1960s. I had a once-in-a-lifetime experience here on this 'Cradle of Christianity' when I felt God saying He wanted a new cradling: the church would be a pilgrim people who are close to God in nature, in the population, in the unseen world of saints and angels, travelling light, with room for hospitality in their hearts. On being assured that the Vicar, David Adam (Vicar 1990–2003) would welcome a presence it was agreed that a few community members should live here in the simplicity of the Island's rhythms and as part of the Island's church life. 'The Open Gate' tries to serve as a home for members, a public retreat house which offers spiritual guidance to pilgrims, and its foyer offers resources. The many Norwegian groups and members who stay are part of the Island's reviving links with Norway. The week-day Midday and Night Prayers in the cellar chapel are open to all. The dispersed community's office, and pilgrim's study library are housed at Lindisfarne retreat cottage. Summer schools and spiritual formation programmes for groups are offered.

The Northumbria Community

This group is not centred on the Island, but at Hetton Hall, a few miles inland. But four of its members live here, including one of the founding members, Andy Raine. Three other members live on the mainland but come to Sunday services at St Mary's church whenever the tide allows, and two of these are on our Parochial Church Council.

This community also has a central house but many dispersed members. It seeks to re-discover something of the gifts of early monasticism in the life of prayer and of mission and to apply these in a 'new monastic' style, and so to take 'the torch of the gospel' out to the people of our generation in whatever ways God makes available. Through its members it is part of the Island story.

Education

Up to 1966 the Island school was all-age, so that Island children had all their schooling there. The 1944 Education Act had made education free and compulsory and raised the school leaving age to 15 years. In 1966 our school became a Primary school, up to the age of 11, and in 1975, when Northumberland changed its system, it became a First School taking children up to the age of nine.

When I came to the Island in 1978 there were about 18 children in the school, taught by a headteacher and a part-time assistant. Gradually the numbers went down to the point where the school could no longer function on its own. It was decided to bring it into closer contact with the nearest First School on the mainland at Lowick, about ten miles away. As it happened, the headteacher at Lowick was leaving and the headteacher here was appointed to be head of both schools.

So began a relationship, now a federation, which has been of great benefit. The head teacher continued to live in the school house here until she retired; then an assistant teacher was appointed to the Island, with the headteacher (of both schools) at Lowick. When the times of the tides make it possible at the beginning and end of the school session our children are taken by car to Lowick, to join in with the school there, and our teacher goes also. But when that is not possible because of tides our children are taught by our own teacher in the school here. So some weeks they spend a lot of time in Lowick and some weeks much less. Of course, it needs very close co-operation between the teachers to make the joint curriculum run smoothly. But for our children the gains are great. Some of the time they have a lot of individual attention here. At other times they have the experience of meeting more children and teachers and working in a bigger setting. Not that Lowick school is large: it is currently 30-plus pupils and our own numbers recently have been between six and ten.

Some very good things have been done by the two schools jointly. A joint sports day is held on the field here; a joint Christmas play is performed in our church here; there are many other joint school activities and excursions.

But at nine years old the Lowick children will go to the Middle School at Berwick and, at 13, on to Berwick High School. In past years our children did the same (except that there were two other Middle Schools our parents could choose if they wished, and a few families did). Holy Island maintained a hostel for its children at Berwick and they went as weekly boarders, living in the hostel during the week, going to the Berwick schools from there, and coming back to the Island at weekends. But when there were very few or no children of this age for a few years that hostel had to be closed. Then the numbers began to creep up again. But without the hostel what would the children do? The tide prevented them from simply coming home every day. Even if the parents were able to go at some later point in each evening to bring them home there was still the problem of what the children would do, where they would go, while they waited, since the Middle and High Schools could not supervise them after the end of the school day.

The solution for this which is being tried and has been running for three years is that the Island children, at nine, should go to a day/boarding school on the edge of Berwick. The fees are paid by the local authority or by bursaries, not by the parents. The parents can collect their children in the evenings if they wish and the children are safe until they come. But the boarding facilities are available. The scheme is still in its early years, but seems to be working well.

Meanwhile, for our First School yet another federation has been made, with Ellingham First School. So the three schools are now under one headteacher. As I write this arrangement is just beginning, but it is clearly a way for small country schools to broaden the opportunities for activities and relationships which can be offered to the pupils.

The lifeboats since 1939

From 1939 the use of the lifeboat from Holy Island began to decline. Between 1940 and 1946 the *Milburn* was launched six times and rescued 30 people. In 1947 it was replaced by the *Gertrude*, which made nine rescues before it was withdrawn and the station was closed by the RNLI in 1968.

Many of the Island people were unhappy at its closure and at the end of a great tradition. Recently there has been a suggestion that the Island should have a 'lifeboat museum', probably to be situated in the old boathouse on the beach opposite St Cuthbert's Island. This would house a genuine lifeboat, such as the *Lizzie Porter* if she could be returned. (But this seems unlikely, as she is now rather a showpiece in a RNLI exhibition.) So the museum might hold an exhibition with perhaps models, charts and so on of the Island's lifeboat story.

This suggestion has been well received and is now in the early planning stage.

Celebration days: two royal visits

Some days live for ever in the memories of those who were there, and this seems to be true of the visit of the Queen and the Duke of Edinburgh on Sunday 19 June 1958. It was the first time that a reigning monarch had come to the Island since Anglo-Saxon days, and the kings who came in those days were kings of Northumbria, not of Great Britain. This visit was at the suggestion of the Vicar of the day, the Revd T. J. Martin, who describes it in great detail in his booklet *A Brief History of the Holy Island of Lindisfarne*. On a beautiful summer's morning the royal yacht *Britannia* approached the Island and the royal barge brought the visitors on to the Island itself. The Queen wore an ice-blue corded silk coat and a pale blue silk hat. Mr Martin gives full lists of those who were presented to the Queen at each stage of her visit. She and the Duke attended Morning Prayer (it was Sunday) at the Parish Church, inspected a guard of honour in Sanctuary Close, were shown round the Priory and saw the newly completed statue of St Aidan by Miss Kathleen Parbury. Two more sycamore trees were planted, using the same spade the Queen's grandparents had used. She visited the Castle and then came back to the Herring Houses, where the Island's Grand Old Lady, Mrs Sally Cromarty, aged 93, was presented. Then back to the fishermen's pier, the barge and the *Britannia*.

At various points gifts were offered: Margaret Drysdale on behalf of the children gave a piece of pottery; Mr John Tough, a disabled Islander, gave a willow basket he had made; the fishermen gave 28 live lobsters in a large box specially made by Mr Ralph Dawson of Seahouses. It was felt to have been a very happy visit.

In the afternoon the Queen's day was completed by a visit to the Farnes. Mr Jack Shiel, father of Jack and Billy, took her on a tour of the islands, including following the route of Grace Darling and her father during their memorable rescue. She gave Mr Shiel a photograph of the royal family, and Sir John Craster gave her a half-box of the famous Craster kippers.

Fifty years later, on 26 June 2008, we had a visit by Prince Edward, Earl of Wessex. One of the really big differences from 50 years earlier was the large amount of security for this visit, indicating a big and sad change in the world's level of anxiety. For

example, only a handful of people were allowed into the churchyard where he planted a tree (using the same spade), and only the
Vicar was allowed to accompany him into the church. However,
lots of people gathered in the Market Square, including the children from the school, and he won everybody's heart by his sheer
friendliness and informality. He arrived by helicopter and went
first to the Castle, then to the Lindisfarne Centre, then through
the Market Square to the churchyard, the church and the Priory.
The visit was short but happy, and then the Prince departed by
helicopter for his next engagement. So in 2058 . . . who?

The Holy Island Community Development Trust

There is always a danger, when a place attracts a huge number
of visitors, that the needs of the local residents and the ordinary life of the village will be pushed into the background. The
Holy Island Development Trust was the inspiration of the late
Ian McGregor and his colleague in this, Richard Patterson. Its
aim is to initiate and carry out projects which are for the benefit
of the Island people. Any profit it makes will be spent for Island
improvements.

The Trust was founded in 1996. The first project was the
building of five houses, of two or three bedrooms, for lease at
affordable rates to younger people who wish to live and work on
the Island. When Island cottages come on the market they are
usually expensive, and the problem for such younger people was
to find housing rather than to find work. Planning restrictions
do not allow any new building outside the boundaries of the
present village, so a piece of land between houses was bought
with the aid of fund-giving charities. These houses are not for
sale, and the first tenancies were allocated with the help of an
external authority. I think there has been a general sense of satisfaction with the way in which that has worked out. This project
was completed by 1999.

The second project was the conversion of the old Castle Hotel
into what was first called the Lindisfarne Heritage Centre and

is now called simply the Lindisfarne Centre to avoid confusion
with English Heritage. The visitor enters first a shop with suitable
books, cards and gifts with connections with the Island's past.
Beyond that is a museum with several rooms. The innermost is
called the 'Gospels Room' as it houses the facsimile of the Lindisfarne Gospels very kindly given to us by the British Library, and
provides information on all aspects of this manuscript. There is
a new Viking room, to pay attention to the attack in 793 which
had a major effect on our history. There are also displays about
aspects of Island life past and present, bird life and so on. The
Centre also acts as an information bureau for visitors.

The upstairs of the old Castle Hotel gave more space for
'affordable housing' and two flats were created there.

The next project was the 'Gospels Garden'. Almost next door
to the Post Office in the main street used to be some allotments
which had fallen out of use. This is now the site of a garden
where the arrangement of flowers and shrubs recalls the art of
the Lindisfarne Gospels. The garden is well used by people who
want to sit for a little while in peace.

Further affordable housing is planned as a questionnaire to
Island residents revealed a further demand. A section of a large
garden was bought and plans are now well advanced for the
construction of four further houses.

The harbour area was donated to the Trust and discussions
are underway about its development now that the Island people
can be sure that it will not be acquired by a commercial devel-
oper. The needs of the Island fishermen will come first here.

So it is hoped that many successful projects will be completed
in the future.

The Monastic Garden

In the previous section I mentioned the 'Gospels Garden' in the
main street. Another garden, the 'Monastic Garden', is the strip
of land outside the churchyard against the west wall, next to
the path going down to St Cuthbert's Island. Until recently this

was just a rough bank until one man, Richard Binns, had the inspiration that this could become a garden growing the plants that would have been in a monastery garden when our second monastery was flourishing. He did the research, obtained the plants, dug and planted the site and, when he is on the Island, keeps it in order. A leaflet about this garden is available in the parish church.

Present practicalities

Currently tourism is the major industry, accounting for 70–80 per cent of the Island's income. About 50 per cent of the housing is not continuously occupied, but this includes cottages which are owned by Island families and let out to supplement the family income, and properties which are owned by friends of the Island who come regularly.

The major organizations are the National Trust, which owns the Castle and has a shop in the village; English Heritage, which owns the Priory and the Priory Museum; English Nature, which owns most of the dunes and the beaches. The Lord of the Manor, Colonel Crossman, owns the farming land and various properties. The parish owns the church and the churchyard. In the village many of the houses are owner-occupied.

The traditional industries of fishing and farming are still practised. Currently there are six working fishing boats and 12 men in the fishermen's society. But of course fishing all over the country is restricted and now our fishermen's main catch is crab and lobster. There are two farms, worked by separate families, and producing sheep, barley, and some fruit and vegetables.

Others among the working population are the Vicar, the Post Office staff, the school teacher and school caretaker, those who run the other church organizations and visitor attractions, and all who staff shops, cafes, hotels and guest houses. There are a fair number of retired people.

The Island has its own little monthly newspaper, the *Holy Island Times*. This began as a supplement to the Deanery church magazine, but has developed into a community periodical, and some who are frequent visitors like to receive it by post every month as a way of keeping in touch.

Finally, a point which we hope all visitors will keep in mind. *The sea is dangerous.* The causeway is not at all dangerous to those who consult the tide-tables and keep their eyes open. But the tide is not a water-splash. 'Racing the tide' is a sport for experts only. The sea must be allowed to have the last word!

And the future?

Who knows? But this chapter will have shown how much liveliness there is here on the Island, how much willingness to accommodate new ventures, but also how much determination there is for the future to be shaped by and for the Island people. We are not ready to become anyone's theme-park, now or ever!

But if you have never been, come and visit. If you have the choice come, not in July or August, but in June or September. If you have already been in spring or autumn come in winter. The days are short, but often dry and bright. The winds can be exhilarating! To me the Island is most beautiful in winter, most itself in its bleakness and stillness. As a winter afternoon begins to darken, walk by the sea or into the dunes and then, if you are at all imaginatively minded, the past will live again.

For Further Reading

 Do let me persuade you to read Bede! He is the indispensable source of the story up to his death in 735. For us his major work is *The Ecclesiastical History of the English People*. This is easily obtainable, in paperback in good modern translations, in the Oxford World Classics Series and in the Penguin Classics Series. Bede's *Life of Cuthbert* is contained in another of the Penguin Classics, *The Age of Bede*. The same book has a translation of Eddius Stephanus' *Life of Wilfrid*. While you are reading sources don't miss, also in Penguin Classics, Richard Sharpe's edition of Adomnan's *Life of Columba*, which will give the feel of Iona and some background to Aidan. Unfortunately the anonymous *Life of Cuthbert* is not so easy to obtain. But ask a library for *Two Lives of St Cuthbert*, edited by Bertram Colgrave and published by the Cambridge University Press, 1940 and (paperback) 1985.

Books on Holy Island: a good factual account is by R. A. and D. B. Cartwright, *The Holy Island of Lindisfarne and the Farne Islands*, published by David and Charles, 1976. However, the reader should be aware that there have been many changes in practical matters since this book was published. For an archaeological account read *Lindisfarne: Holy Island* by D. O'Sullivan and R. Young, published by English Heritage, 1995. The authors were archaeologists from Leicester University who with their students excavated on the Island during many annual visits. A very readable account by an Islander is Charles Cromarty's *The Lindisfarne Story*, published by Frank Graham, 1971. Many people have enjoyed Magnus Magnusson's *Lindisfarne: the Cradle Island*, Oriel Press, 1984. This is now available in paperback, but do if possible get the original hardback from the library and appreciate Sheila Mackie's illustrations.

If you yearn for some solid history wider in scope than the Island try Henry Mayr-Harting, *The Coming of Christianity to Anglo-Saxon England*, Batsford, 1991, and David Rollason, *Northumbria 500–1100*, Cambridge University Press, 2003.

But also . . . please read Bede!

Index

Lightning Source UK Ltd.
Milton Keynes UK
UKOW04n1258091014

239848UK00010B/140/P